HOW TO HEAR GOD SPEAK

by
Charles Wesley Bush

IMPACT BOOKS, INC.
KIRKWOOD, MO.

> Editorial Statement: Impact Books, Inc.
>
> The manuscript for this book has been prayerfully edited by our staff. It is our belief that this book will be helpful to *every* believer who approaches it in an attitude of prayer and openness.
>
> It is our prayer that it may contribute to making each of us more sensitive, receptive, and hopefully, attuned to Hear God Speak *to us!*
>
> Editor

COVER DESIGN: Barry E. Newcomb

© COPYRIGHT 1975
IMPACT BOOKS, INC.
137 W. JEFFERSON AVE.,
KIRKWOOD, MO. 63122

All Rights Reserved

PRINTED IN THE UNITED STATES OF AMERICA

Contents

SECTION I
Hearing God

1. Why Hear God Speak? 3
2. How To Be Sure It Is God Speaking 8
3. One Promise From God Is Sufficient 12
4. Letting God Speak Audibly 16
5. Expressing Our Love By Hearing
   And Obeying God 19

SECTION II
Hearkening to God

6. The Difference Between Hearing
   And Hearkening 25
7. A Proper Pattern For Prayer 29
8. Hearing And Obeying God
   Could Save Your Life 33
9. Good Confessions Are God's Confessions.. 38
10. How Mistakes Might Arise
    In Trying To Hear God 43
11. The Price Of Ignoring God 47

SECTION III
Benefits of Hearing God

12. The Blessing Of Following God 51

13. Total Victory Follows
     Listening And Obeying 54
14. What We May Ask And Expect
     To Receive 62
15. Hearing God Speak Peace
     Concerning Lost Loved Ones 65
16. How Your Hearing God Affects Others... 70
17. How Hearing God Relates
     To Spiritual Gifts 76

SECTION IV
God Speaking Through Prophecy

18. Who Should Prophesy? 83
19. Where Does Prophecy Come From? 84
20. Pre-Testing Your Own Prophecy 86
21. How You May Prophesy 92
22. Stumbling Blocks To Prophesying 94
23. Why Prophesy? 97

SECTION V
God Speaking Through Power (Fire)

24. About The Fire 101
25. Search For The Fire 104
26. How To Find The Fire 110
27. Conclusion In Faith 114
28. Key Questions And Answers 116

ABOUT THE AUTHOR

Wes Bush entered part-time service to the Lord in 1969, less than 2 years after being Baptised in the Holy Spirit. His first effort, still going strong, is a non-profit organization: The Lee McAlister Foundation, begun to provide tapes for shut-ins.

Since 1971 when Wes and his family left the construction business, they have been engaged in full time ministry. Their multi-faceted ministry includes teaching, preaching, convention recording and book displays, providing a cassette library (over 1000 tapes available on an exchange basis) and a complete bookstore on wheels to serve small communities.

As you read this book, you will see the exciting ways God has been able to use this ministry. . . .

FOR FURTHER INFORMATION, WRITE:
 WES BUSH/LEE McALISTER
  FOUNDATION
 P. O. BOX 5767
 ARLINGTON, TEXAS 76011

SECTION I

Hearing God

CHAPTER 1

Why Hear God Speak?

The importance of hearing God's voice can never be overstated, as we must communicate with Him if we are to be able to obey Him.

The argument that because we now have the perfect word, (the Bible) we no longer need to talk to God, carries little weight with one who is lost and needs direction from the Lord. So long as men are men they will find themselves face to face with real situations that demand decisions that are beyond their ability to make and make correctly. A little conversation with God can bring His answer and a clear and correct decision.

As we read God's written word, we gain knowledge of the many wonderful things God has done, can do, and will do; but, when God's Holy Spirit speaks to us, we are inspired to believe that what He has done for those in His written word, He *will do for us!* By listening to Him, we have the verbal answers to our prayers before we see the physical evidence, and thereby enjoy great peace.

I was desperate to sell a house one day and needed relief from the mental anguish I was suffering because I had seen no signs that the house was going to sell. The notes were due and something had to happen in order to divert my impending doom.

My mother and I agreed in prayer and asked God to send a buyer through His supernatural power. He spoke through my mother, and said, "I have heard your prayer and I have established the answer for I have a buyer on the way and it will be done this day." A few hours later, that same day we sold the house. Had I known how to listen as I do now, I could have prayed for the (verbal) answer days before, and God would have told me to be patient and to trust Him for He had a buyer prepared and it would be consummated in due season. All my mental anguish could have been avoided.

Although the written Word of God is limited to giving us the knowledge of our blessings and privileges in God and of the penalties for moving outside the framework of His will as set forth in the Bible, rather than giving us moment by moment instructions to guide our every footstep; we dare not set it aside and rely only upon the presently spoken Word of God, lest we open the door for Satan to mislead us.

The Bible is one sure and certain authority to which we may turn for verification of the expediency of those words we receive as present direction from God and we have sure knowledge that no presently spoken word of God will in any way set aside, alter or change the already empiracle, unalterable precepts God has so clearly delineated in His written Word.

In this behalf we speak to all who are young in the Lord, and admonish them to seek the written Word of God diligently, studying to show themselves approved—workmen rightly dividing the word of truth and to shun profane and vain babblings! for they will increase unto more ungodliness. II Tim. 2:15-16.

This is not to say that a new-born babe in Christ should not attempt to hear God speak, and to be willing to act upon the guidance he receives from the Lord. It *is* to say, that he need be careful to test every word he receives in light of the Scripture, to be certain that it is within the framework of God's perfect will (written word.)

Only as one matures in knowledge and understanding of God's written Word can he become completely at ease in his conversational relationship with God; and, even then, he must continually read and re-read, study and re-study the Scripture, lest he forget a portion and thereby be snared by deception.

The Psalmist declared, "Blessed are the undefiled in the way, who walk in the law of the Lord. Blessed are they that keep his testimonies, and that seek him with the whole heart. They also do no iniquity: they walk in his ways.

"Thou hast commanded us to keep thy precepts diligently. Oh that my ways were directed to keep thy statutes! Then shall I not be ashamed, when

I have respect unto all thy commandments. I will praise thee with uprightness of heart, when I shall have learned thy righteous judgements. I will keep thy statutes: O forsake me not utterly.

"Wherewithal shall a young man cleanse his way? by taking heed thereto according to thy word. With my whole heart have I sought thee: O let me not wander from thy commandments. *Thy WORD have I hid in mine heart, that I might not sin against thee.* Blessed art thou, O Lord: teach me thy statutes.

"With my lips have I declared all the judgements of thy mouth. I have rejoiced in the way of thy testimonies, as much as in all riches. I will meditate in thy precepts, and have respect unto thy ways. I will delight myself in thy statutes: *I will not forget thy word.*" Psalms 119:1-16.

These beautiful words of the Psalmist express the deep need we have to continually meditate upon God's Word, fitting everything we think or do into His perfect will thereby. What a tremendous privilege it is to read God's matchless precepts, but how much more glorious to hear His voice speak, confirming that those precepts apply to one's personal life.

I would again caution the young in Christ to be careful to test the spirits and to move slowly and deliberately into this relationship with God, just as a young child must spend much time practicing the use of words before he gains sufficient knowledge to grasp the deeper things of life as they are spoken to him by others.

Young Samuel reveals the necessity of learning or growing into conversational relationship with God. In I Samuel 3:1-10, we read,

"And the child Samuel ministered unto the Lord before Eli. And the word of the Lord was precious in those days; there was no open vision.

"And it came to pass at that time, when Eli was laid down in his place, and his eyes began to wax dim, that he could not see; And ere the lamp of God went out in the temple of the Lord, where the ark of God was, and Samuel was laid down to sleep; That the Lord called Samuel: and he answered, Here am I.

"And he ran to Eli, and said, Here am I; for thou calledst me." And he said, "I called not; lie down again." And he went and lay down.

"And the Lord called yet again, Samuel." And Samuel arose and went to Eli, and said, "Here am I; for thou didst call me." And he answered, "I called not, my son, lie down again."

"Now Samuel did *not yet know the Lord, neither was the word of the Lord, yet revealed unto him.* And the Lord called Samuel again the third time. And he arose and went to Eli, and said, "Here am I; for thou didst call me." And Eli perceived that the Lord had called the child.

"Therefore Eli said unto Samuel, "Go, lie down: and it shall be, if he call thee, that thou shalt say,

Speak, Lord, for thy servant heareth." So Samuel went and lay down in his place.

"And the Lord came, and stood, and called as at other times, "Samuel, Samuel." Then Samuel answered, "Speak; for thy servant heareth."

If one so greatly anointed and used of God as was Samuel had to *grow* into this conversational relationship, surely it is not too much to expect that we must also learn to know the voice of the Lord before we can begin to properly respond.

CHAPTER 2

How To Be Sure It Is God Speaking

My conversational relationship with God began while I was praying one morning. The Lord began to instruct me by His Spirit, and I realized that he was really *TALKING* to me!

He said to me, "Son, why do you not listen to me so I can instruct you in the way to receive that which you desire of me, and in the pathway you are to go?"

I exclaimed, "But Lord, how do I know it is you and not just my vain imagination or some spirit other than the Holy Spirit speaking to me?"

He replied, "Let me show you. My word says: 'Ask and it shall be given you; seek, and ye shall find; knock, and it shall be opened unto you. For one that asketh receiveth; and he that seeketh findeth; and to him that knocketh it shall be opened. Or, what man is there of you, whom if his son ask bread, will he give him a stone? Or if he ask a fish, will he give him a serpent? If ye then, being evil, know how to give good gifts unto your children, how much more shall your Father which is in heaven give good things to them that ask him? (Mt. 7:7-11) Can't you see that when you speak to me and you invite me to speak to you, *I will not let another speak in my stead;* but I will always be faithful to answer you that you may freely receive that which I desire for you?"

I realized then that I must accept this promise of God and never doubt that He would answer when I asked Him to speak, nor would He allow another spirit to answer me first. I knew that were I to ever assume otherwise, I would be calling God a liar and I would become confused beyond measure.

God continued speaking, saying, "Just consider the possible avenues I might use to heal a backache were you to ask for such a healing. Consider also that if you failed to listen to me and follow my instructions, you might not receive the healing which is already yours by inheritance. Consider that I might desire to be glorified *to* the local chiropractor through your backache, and were this so, I would instruct you to call him and say, 'God told me that He has anointed your hands to heal my back* and I would like an appointment please'. Now you know he is going to think you are crazy, but that won't stop him from giving you an appointment, for he wants your business. Being a good chiropractor, he will refuse to touch your back until he has given you a thorough examination and has x-rayed your back to determine the trouble. The x-rays will clearly show that you have two cracked discs and he knows that he does not have the ability to correct them. Therefore, he will recommend that you go to a specialist for surgery.

"Then you say, 'No, God said that he had anointed *your hands* to heal my back, so if you don't mind, just go ahead and give me a regular treatment, please.' knowing that a normal treatment might further injure your back, he will be very careful and will just make you believe that he is treating you by manipulating your back gently rather than bending and popping the spine as he would normally do. Can you imagine his tremendous surprise when this simple manipulation produces a complete and total healing in you? I will have been glorified through your backache because he will know that I am God and that I am working today as I did from the beginning.

---

*These words from the Lord did not convey to the author anything of significance as concerns doctors. God did not imply that he either always uses doctors in the miracle of healing, nor did He imply that He does not use doctors. The full import of this instruction to me was that *I* must hear God's direction, hearken to it, and obey it, or *I could not* expect to be recipient of His blessings.

"Now, on the other hand, I might say to you, 'Straighten up, sit straight, walk straight, and carry yourself erect. A correct posture will cause your backache to disappear'; or, I might even say to you, 'Arise and be made whole, for your faith has made you whole'.

"Can you see how it is that you have become frustrated in times past because you have not hearkened to my voice and obeyed my instructions and have had evil come upon you because of it? Hearken to me and obey me and I will surely instruct you in all rightness and in every good thing."

Oh, praise God, what a wonderful lesson He had given me, for now I could approach my Father confidently and receive His instruction and never doubt that it was Him doing the speaking.

He said, "My sheep *hear* my voice, and I know them, and they follow me: and I give unto them eternal life; and they shall never perish, neither shall any man pluck them out of my hand. My father, which gave them me, is greater than all; and no man is able to pluck them out of my father's hand. I and my father are one."

John 10:27-30

What a tremendous promise! What a tremendous blessing! What a tremendous assurance He has given those who know Him and whom He knows!

CHAPTER 3

One Promise From God Is Sufficient

Some might ask for more scripture than Jesus' own promise, "If you know how to give good gifts to your children, how much more will the Heavenly father give the Holy Spirit to them that ask him", to show that the very first voice we hear must be the voice of God when we have asked God specifically to speak to us by His Holy Spirit.

My answer to this is that there is only one formula, $1+1+1+1=4$, and, any other statement of mathematics that ends in the product 4 is but a restatement of that formula.

We have a clear statement from Jesus that God will not deceive us nor allow us to be deceived as long as we pray in faith and stand in faith. Any other statement that the scripture might make that ends in the same product would serve only as a restatement of that same promise.

As laymen we are not so much concerned with why $1+1+1+1=4$ as we are in the use of the formula (in faith) to serve our needs. Likewise, we should be more interested in using the promises of God than in proving them.

I was in Frederick, Oklahoma and my finances were in poor shape. It was close to the end of the month and I was $600.00 short of having enough to pay the bills for the month and I was feeling the pressure.

My custom is to go to Vernon, Texas from Frederick, and share with a prayer group there and this had been my plan when I began the trip, but I had not sold enough books to meet my needs and I had never had much business in Vernon, so I asked God if I should miss Vernon and go somewhere else instead.

The Lord said, "No, my son, I want you to go to Vernon tomorrow and share with my people. I will work a work through you and I will meet your need before tomorrow night is past."

The next day I drove expectantly into Vernon, just knowing that I would do a lot of business. As the day wore on it became more and more clear that I was not going to sell any books. The wind was blowing very hard and it was cold and dusty. No one was interested in books. They wanted shelter!

I closed the store* in time to pull it to the prayer group, and I was thinking to myself that I surely must not have heard God right. Then He spoke again and said, "Doubt not in thine heart that you have heard me right, for I will meet your

---

*Lee McAlister Foundation sponsors a complete traveling Christian bookstore, used to minister to small communities which do not have access to Christian books and church aids.

need this night. Speak to my people concerning how they too might hear me speak and I will surely bless you."

I thought to myself, "Praise God, there must be going to be a huge crowd of people there who will buy a lot of books, if God is to supply $600.00 by midnight". To my amazement, the crowd was only about 12 to 14 people, and I just knew I could not possibly receive my need from so small a number. I must have heard God wrong, and He had told me to speak on how to hear Him speak. My heart was willing, but my flesh was weak. How could I speak on how to hear God speak when I was in the midst of wondering if I could truly hear Him anymore myself?

As the meeting progressed and it came time for me to share, it became more and more obvious that the Holy Spirit had directed the service in the channel that demanded that I speak on 'How to Hear God Speak', so by faith, I began to talk. To my surprise, God filled my mouth with words and my heart with faith, and poured forth a lesson that was beneficial and fresh even to me.

After the meeting I opened the book trailer and as the people came through, buying $1.00 or $2.00 each, I became puzzled as to how God would perform the $600.00 miracle.

A young man and his wife, who were visitors at the meeting, came into the trailer as everyone else left. He said, "Brother Bush, you just don't know how much God has used you to help us tonight. My wife and I have been desperately seeking God's guidance for the last three months. I was a career officer in the Service and intended to retire as an officer. However, a few months ago I was separated from the service without notice as a part of President Nixon's "rift" program. Since then we have been seeking God for an answer as to what we are to do. Now, I know that we have been hearing God speak to us all the time, but we were attributing it to our imagination. Now I know His desire for us and I have the direction I have been seeking." He then handed me a check and said, "This is part of the tithe on my separation pay, and I want you to have it."

Praise be to the name of the Lord! It was in the amount of $600.00. How my heart rejoiced and shouted, "Hallelujah! Glory to His Holy Name!"

After arriving home from this trip, I began to write my expense checks and found that I had made an error in estimating my needs. Instead of $600.00 my immediate requirements were for $700.00 I had only just discovered this, when my eldest son who had been vacuum cleaning the trailer came rushing in, shouting, "Hey, Dad, I bet you didn't know this was in the donation box in the trailer!" He handed me a folded check in the amount of $100.00 It was from the couple who sponsor the share group at Vernon, and had been deposited quietly in the donation box the same night I was in Vernon. God had anticipated my need and had faithfully performed His word.

Some who read about this will doubt, some will believe and receive; others will try to prove God cautiously; and others will flatly refuse to believe and will criticize those of us who do.

The question is not what someone else is doing with these truths, but rather what are *you* doing with them? Are you going to step out on His promises and receive, in spite of the fact that you may risk failure? Or are you going to avoid any risk of failure by not obtaining the promise and forfeiting the unmatchable benefits?

One never has to look far for criticism, and I have had my share as I have taught upon this subject. However, those who criticize flounder in the pit of despair trying to reason their way out of problems while God has whispered sweet peace to me, giving me joy and peace in the midst of the problem.

Won't *you* talk to God today?

CHAPTER 4

Letting God Speak Audibly

While I was praying one morning, God said to me, "Wes, you have not been fair with me." I said, "How so Lord?"

He asked, "Do you know the scripture that says

'What, know ye not that your bodies are the temple of God, and ye are not your own? for ye are bought with a price; therefore glorify God *in* your body, and *in* your spirit, which are God's?"

"Yes Lord, I know that scripture and I gave you my body a long time ago", I replied.

"If you gave me your body" he asserted, "I would like an answer to this then. Your voice is not you. Your voice is a facility of my temple which I bought and paid for with Jesus's blood. Why is it that you use that voice to pray out loud to me, but you never let me use it *to answer you out loud?"*

Wow, what a bombshell he had dropped on me! What a revelation He had opened to me! I exclaimed, "Oh Lord, I'm sorry! I didn't know you wanted to speak to me *out loud*. I *will* let you speak! I *will* let you use my voice!"

From this moment on I began to yield my voice readily and eagerly to the Lord when conversing with him privately, and I began to realize a singular benefit which can come to a Christian only through this avenue. For the first time I was hearing God in my conscious mind through my ear and for the first time I had the memory banks receiving what He said to me as He said it, instead of having to immediately review the utterances of that still, small voice and try to retain His instructions.

I had come into a fuller realization of the

meaning of Hebrews 8:10-11, wherein God declares:

> "This is the covenant that I will make with the house of Israel after those days, saith the Lord; I will put my laws into their mind, and write them in their hearts: and I will be to them a God, and they shall be to me a people: and they shall not teach every man his neighbor, and every man his brother, saying, Know the Lord; for all shall know me from the least to the greatest."

For the first time I fully realized that the house of Israel no longer needed to rely on the voice of the prophet to *hear* God speak to them and to intimately know Him, but rather, *now* could hear Him speak even through the voice of the hearer that the individual within the house of Israel might truly *know* God and His direction for their individual lives.

Unnecessary, you say? Most certainly not, for almost anyone who hears God speak in the still small voice will testify that they hear him, but so often immediately forget His instruction before being able to obey Him; but, when His words come to the mind through both the Spirit and audible sound; then it is possible to retain what He says and thereby be enabled to obey His words.

I praise God that He made me aware of this new covenant and I continually ask Him to:

"Speak, Oh Lord that this temple might be shaken by the sound of your voice.

"Speak, Oh Lord, that all who thirst might be invited to come freely to the fountain of its waters and drink their fill.

"Speak, Oh Lord, that all who hath an ear might hear."

Amen

CHAPTER 5

Expressing Our Love By Hearing And Obeying God

I know now that I had been hearing the voice of God for many years, but I had always assumed that it was my own imagination, or that maybe even Satan could be trying to trick me. Praise be to the Father for showing me that when I ask Him to speak and not let me hear any other voice, He *will not allow* another to answer me.

Oh how sweet is the sound of that still small voice as it speaks ever so softly in my spirit; but, with such grace and authority that I am now *ashamed that I ever assumed I had intellect enough to imagine such,* for His wisdom and beauty is beyond measure!

What great power and authority are manifested

when I yield my voice to Him and I hear that still small voice amplified to speak through this temple's "public address system" those words of wisdom, knowledge, and faith, that only my Father can express in just that way.

Have you made room for Him in the temple you inhabit? I exhort you to open the door wide to Him. Let His light wash it clean and illuminate it, and let Him use all its facilities.

Fellowship with Him and converse with Him. You will grow to love Him as never before, for He says, "Behold, I stand at the door and knock, if any man hear my voice, and opens the door, I will come in to him, and will sup with him, and he with me." Rev. 3-20

"If a man love me, he will keep *my* words: and my father will love him, and we will come unto him, and make our abode with him." John 14:23-24.

Are you keeping His words or are you doing as I was doing; talking but not listening? Listen to His words and obey them, and He and the Father will surely take up residence in your temple as He has in mine.

"And the comforter, which is the Holy Ghost, whom the Father will send in my name, he shall teach you all things, and bring all things to your remembrance, whatsoever I have said unto you. Peace I give unto you. Not as the world giveth, give I unto you. Let not your heart be troubled, neither let it be afraid."

John 14:26-27

Of all the apparent truths contained in the Bible, the most apparent are that God surely does talk to man and that those men who listen and obey are the ones who have the great experiences and relationships with God.

Won't you talk to Him today?

SECTION II

Hearkening To God

CHAPTER 6

The Difference Between Hearing And Hearkening

One night as I was on my way to a meeting in Altus, Oklahoma, the joy of the Lord was flowing full and free. Songs of praise, psalms, and hymns were flowing out of me in truly exuberant fashion as I sang and praised the Lord.

I was somewhere between Lawton, Oklahoma and Altus, when I passed a sign at a crossroad which pointed the way to Frederick, Oklahoma, and the thought went fleeting through my mind, "Why don't you go to Frederick?" I just kept on driving and singing, not paying any attention to that thought. I heard it, you see, but I didn't hearken to it.

That was Thursday night. I had planned to park our mobile book trailer in Altus Friday and sell books to the public, and then speak for a large home prayer group Friday night. I was scheduled to open the bookstore to the public again Saturday and speak for the Full Gospel Businessmen's Fellowship that night.

Previously when I had prayed about this schedule (about a month earlier) I had received a word from God that I should go to Altus for the two meetings; but I had not received any details as to where or when to open the traveling bookstore.

When I arrived in Altus about 9:30 Thursday night, I was full of the joy of the Lord (who could praise the Lord in psalms and hymns and spiritual songs for several hours without filling with the joy of the Lord?) and I was confident that I was right where He wanted me to be. I went to bed early without letting God speak instructions to me.

When I awakened, I began to talk to God, as is my custom, and I asked, "Lord, should I drive downtown and let you point out a parking place for me or should I call Duane Olson, the president of the Full Gospel Businessmen's Chapter, and let him direct me to a parking place?"

To my surprise, He replied, "I tried to get your attention last night to tell you that you aren't supposed to be in Altus this morning; you should be in Frederick. I have a man there that I want you to minister to. You will know him when he enters the book trailer, and I will give you the words to say." He then made me aware that I would park at an intersection that would have a restaurant on one corner, a grocery store across the street from it, a service station on another corner, and a public building of some kind across from the station.

He went on to say, "You are to leave now and go to Frederick, and I will have the people prepared to receive you, and I will bless your finances.

You could have saved 30 miles of driving had you hearkened to me last night."

I obeyed God, went to Frederick and guess where I parked? The first signal light I came to was an intersection at which was a restaurant, a grocery store, a service station, and the County Courthouse. There was plenty of open space at the courthouse and I parked there for the day.

My business flourished and I met many wonderful people. God blessed my finances and I was waiting expectantly when, at 4:00 in the afternoon, a young man came into the trailer, and I knew he was the one, to whom God had sent me. God ministered some truths to him which blessed him greatly and moved him into a fresh dimension with God. I was then free to return to Altus for my evening prayer and share group. How wonderful is the Lord and how matchless are His ways.

I could have saved 30 miles of driving and gotten to bed sooner if I had hearkened to God the night before. I should have known that it was He speaking because all my thoughts were directed toward Him, and Satan had no place to reside.

When our thoughts are centered on God, He is sure to be directing our thoughts, for Jesus said, "I am the *way*, the *truth*, and the life: No man cometh unto the Father, but by me." (John 14:6).

Hence, we know that when we are spiritually motivated to even ask God for His guidance, that *very motivation itself came from Him;* therefore we can be certain that *He* hears and *He* answers and will not let another voice speak to us, unless we open the door to it by doubting God.

Failure to hearken to God has cost many their lives. God told Saul to utterly destroy the Amalekites, but Saul allowed the people to persuade him to let them keep the best of the Amalekites' possessions as a sacrifice unto the Lord. Although his intentions were good, he had not *hearkened* to God and his disobedience cost him his throne and ultimately his life.

Samuel asked Saul this question concerning his disobedience, "Hath the Lord as great delight in burnt offerings and sacrifices, as in obeying the voice of the Lord? Behold, to obey is better than sacrifice, and to *hearken* than the fat of rams. For rebellion is as the sin of witchcraft, and stubbornness is as iniquity and idolatry." (I Sam. 15:22)

God himself declared, "Put your burnt-offerings unto your sacrifices, and eat flesh. For I spake not unto your fathers, nor commanded them in the day that I brought them out of the land of Egypt, concerning burnt offerings or sacrifices: but this thing commanded I them, saying, Obey my voice, and I will be your God, and ye shall be my people: and walk ye in all the ways that I have commanded you, that it may be well unto you.

"But they *hearkened* not, nor inclined their ear, but walked in the counsels and in the imagination of their evil heart and went backward, and not forward.

"Since the day that your fathers came forth out

of the land of Egypt unto this day I have even sent unto you all my servants the prophets, daily rising up early and sending them: yet they *hearkened* not unto me, nor inclined their ear, but hardened their neck: they did worse than their fathers.

"Therefore thou shalt speak all these words unto them; but they will not *hearken* to thee: thou shalt also call unto them; but they will not answer thee.

"But thou shalt say unto them, this is a nation that obeyeth not the voice of the Lord their God, nor receiveth correction: truth is perished, and is cut off from their mouth.

"Cut off thine hair, O Jerusalem, and cast it away, and take up a lamentation on high places; for the Lord hath rejected and forsaken the generation of his wrath." (Jeremiah 7:21-29)

I declare unto you beloved, that it is extremely important to hear God speak, but equally important to *hearken* to what He says; for to receive His blessing we must *hear Him, hearken to Him, trust Him,* and *obey Him.* But to be separated from His blessing, we need only refuse to *hearken.*

CHAPTER 7

A Proper Pattern For Prayer

Jesus taught us a step by step pattern to follow

in conversing with God, which I have found to be most effective. This pattern is revealed in Matthew 6:9-13.

STEP #1. Recognize the person you are addressing in such a way that there can be no mistake to whom you are talking.

"Our Father which art in heaven." When Jesus opened His prayer with this statement there could be no possibility of mistake concerning whom he was addressing.

We must recognize that we are approaching *our* Father and that He is in Heaven. Jesus said in Matthew 23:9, "And call no man your father upon the earth: for one is your Father, which is in heaven."

STEP #2. Give proper honor, position, and authority to the Father.

a.) "Hallowed be thy name." *His honor is that He is Holy* and cannot change.

Numbers 23:19 declares, "God is not a man, that he should lie; neither the son of man that he should repent". Malachi 3:6 is emphatic as it states, "I am the Lord, I change not."

b.) "Thy kingdom come". In *His position as king*, He is head over all things. There is none higher than the Father.

c.) "Thy will be done on earth as it is in heaven." *His authority as king* demands that His will be done and when we pray this with understanding, we pray in faith that the earth will surely be brought under subjection to our heavenly Father and will become a fit place for His physical kingdom. We are told in Revelation Chapter 20 that an angel will be sent from heaven to bind Satan for a thousand years and that the saints of God will rule and reign with Christ for a thousand years on this earth.

STEP #3. Ask the Father for your needs and desires.

"Give us this day our daily bread." God will surely supply even our most subtle desires if we please him and walk in obedience to him. I John 3:21-22 tells us, "Beloved, if our heart condemn us not, then have we confidence toward God. And *whatsoever* we ask, we receive of him, because we keep his commandments and do those things that are pleasing in his sight."

STEP #4. Forgive those who have come against you and ask that you be forgiven accordingly.

"Forgive us our debts, as we forgive our debtors."

Mathew 6:14-15 tells us, "For if ye forgive men their trespasses, your heavenly Father will also forgive you: but if ye forgive not men their trespasses, neither will your Father forgive your trespasses."

STEP #5. Gain sustenance for your spiritual life by asking to be set free from your faults and evil nature.

"Lead us not into temptation, but deliver us from evil."

I John 1:9 declares, "If we confess our sins, he is faithful and just to forgive us our sins, and to cleanse us from all unrighteousness."

James 5:16 tells us, "Confess your faults one to another, and pray one for another, that ye may be healed."

STEP #6. Re-affirm your respect and honor of the Father and praise Him for the answer that you expect *first to hear* and *then to see*.

"For thine is the kingdom, and the power, and the glory, for ever. Amen."

STEP #7. Meditate upon the Lord and wait patiently to hear His answer.

Since you have asked His Holy Spirit to speak to you, *no other voice will speak;* therefore, *the very first thought you have will be a God-inspired thought*, and if you will speak the words of that thought aloud you will be speaking God's answer to your prayer.

We have Christ's own promise in Matthew 7:7-11 that we can have what we ask. "Ask, and it shall be given you; seek, and ye shall find; knock, and it shall be opened unto you. For every one that asketh receiveth; and he that seeketh findeth; and to him that knocketh it shall be opened.

"Or what man is there of you, whom if his son ask bread, will he give him a stone? Or if he ask a fish, will he give him a serpent? If ye then, being evil, know how to give good gifts unto your children, how much more shall your Father which is in heaven give good things to them that ask him?"

Another place He said, "How much more will the heavenly Father give the Holy Spirit to them that ask him." This is God's empiracle irrevocable promise to you that when you ask His Holy Spirit to speak to you, no other spirit will be allowed to speak. The only way you will hear another voice is to doubt the first voice you hear. When doubt appears, the Holy Spirit becomes silent and you then fall into confusion.

Beloved, believe God. Stand on His promise and be certain that the first voice you hear will be His voice, then when you ask God to speak the answers to your prayers, He will surely speak. You will then have His "Word" on the matter and can be at rest until you see the physical evidence of the answer.

CHAPTER 8

Hearing And Obeying Could Save Your Life

On the morning of January 16, 1974 God spoke to me and gave me instructions that saved my life. Had I not known Him and had I not known His voice I would be dead today.

I was on my way to Fairfield, Texas and had stopped to share with a small church in Oakwood,

Texas on Wednesday evening, January 15, 1974. After the service, a brother asked me to park my motor coach in front of his home and spend the night so we could have coffee and a time of sharing before bedtime. Since his home was on my way, and only 7 miles south of Fairfield, I agreed to do this, and we shared the blessings of the Lord until midnight when I got into the coach to go to bed.

I was confident everything was in perfect working order, for the power-plant which furnishes the electricity for the coach had been overhauled just three days earlier on Monday, and I left it running to be sure that my furnace would have plenty of power, as this was the night of the hardest freeze we were to have during the winter of 1973-74. It was sleeting and the radio had announced that all the roads were icing over and that we should stay off the highways if at all possible. I went to bed at midnight with perfect confidence, and immediately fell into a deep sleep.

I awakened at 5:00 o'clock and looked at my watch, not realizing that anything was amiss, but somewhat puzzled as to why had I awakened, since I normally sleep until 8 or 9 o'clock if I am up late.

The Lord spoke to me in the still small voice, saying, "Son, if you don't go to Fairfield now, you will never make it." I could hear the sleet hitting the tin roof of the motor coach and I thought "But Lord, if it is going to be iced over in the morning, no one will want to come into the bookmobile anyway, so why don't I just stay here in front of my friends' house until the ice thaws?"

In spite of my feelings, I knew better than to disobey God, and so asked Him if he *really* wanted me to go to Fairfield right then. When He began to answer, I let Him use my voice and He said out loud, "Yes son, if you don't go to Fairfield now, you will *never* make it." I knew when He emphasized the word "never" that I had better be up and going.

I rolled out of bed completely unaware that anything was wrong, until I immediately collapsed. There was not an ounce of strength in my body. I struggled and fell, and struggled and fell, cutting my knees and bruising my body until I was finally able to reach the driver's seat and open the window, completely unable to imagine what was happening. As soon as I breathed a breath of the icy cold, fresh air, I realized that I had been breathing exhaust fumes and had been overcome by carbon monoxide. I turned the power plant off with the switch on the instrument panel of the coach and sat, inhaling deeply of the cold, fresh air trying to revive myself.

After approximately 20 minutes I regained sufficient strength to get out of the coach and raise the jacks in order to leave, knowing that I was not to take time to awaken my friend's household but that I was to go to Fairfield now in obedience to God's command.

As I re-entered the coach I became aware that

my bowels had involuntarily emptied before I had awakened and this let me know that I had truly come face-to-face with the Angel of Death.

I managed to get things in order and get dressed, and drove to Fairfield as quickly as possible. I only remember two iced-over bridges along the way. In my memory, I can still see the reflections of the coach's headlights on the glazed floors of the bridges as I very cautiously but nearly unconsciously approached them.

When I arrived at Fairfield, I went to a truck stop that I remembered, thinking I could wait there until morning; but when I drove into the parking lot, I could smell the exhaust emissions of the large trucks which were parked there, and I knew that I could not stay there. I drove back toward town not knowing what to do and God showed me a sign which directed me to the hospital and I knew I was to go there. I barely parked and got inside the front door before I was ready to collapse again. The nurses began to give me oxygen immediately.

I could tell that the doctor and his staff could not really believe I had experienced carbon monoxide poisoning. The doctor said that he couldn't understand it, "for no person in a deep sleep can begin to take carbon monoxide and then awaken, but will just get deeper and deeper asleep until he expires." But you see, the doctor didn't realize who my Father is and that when *He* says to awaken, *the very dead come to life.*

The following day I took the coach back to the same repair shop in Dallas where I'd had it serviced and they discovered that they had left the clamp loose which holds the muffler to the exhaust manifold and that exhaust fumes were escaping in heavy amounts. They had also left an 18" exhaust extension off the end of the exhaust pipe which permitted all the exhaust fumes to collect under the coach. They also found a hole about the size of a large orange between the power plant compartment and the bathroom cabinet through which the exhaust fumes could freely enter the coach.

I had breathed these fumes from 12:00 o'clock midnight until 5:00 A.M. I had apparently expired to the point of emptying my bowels. I had been awakened by God and received His instruction, and I live today because I *heard* Him, *hearkened* to His voice, *trusted* Him and *obeyed* His command. Praise be to His holy name forever!

I know now, as I reflect upon this sequence of events, that had I not allowed God to use my voice the second time He spoke His instruction to me, I would have argued myself out of going at that moment, for the coach was so warm and the bed so comfortable that I had a dread of getting out in the cold to prepare to leave. Had I forced Him to speak in the still small voice the second time, I would have missed the emphasis on the word 'never' and would have assumed that He was still speaking of the icing conditions.

When God is allowed to speak in only the still

small voice, His word is still only spirit; but, when He has spoken the word audibly, the word becomes quickened even more so to us as TRUTH, a valid contract with the universe, which *must* come to pass!

Won't you invite God to talk to you today?

CHAPTER 9

Good Confessions Are God's Confessions

The many faith ministries of today are all agreed that the basis of receiving those things we believe for is to confess that we have them before we see them. They agree that a positive confession is absolutely necessary to activate faith and that faith and fear are diametrically opposed to one another.

You see, we cannot believe we will receive an answer to our prayers and at the same time be afraid that we won't receive the answers. The Bible declares that perfect love casts out fear and, therefore, we must find perfect love to have the ability to positively confess that we have received our answer before we see it materialize.

John tells us how to have that perfect love: "Whosoever shall confess that Jesus is the Son of God, God dwelleth in him, and he in God. And we have known and believed the love that God hath to us. God is love; and he that dwelleth in love dwelleth in God, and God in him. Herein is our love made perfect, that we may have boldness in the day of judgement: because as he is, so are we in this world. There is no fear in love; but perfect love casteth out fear: because fear hath torment. (I John 4:15-18)

What a tremendous, clear and open promise to us. What a wonderful and priceless gift from our Heavenly Father; that when we truly believe that Jesus is the Son of God, we love God and God loves us; and we are as He is and have received that Perfect Love which exercises faith.

Jesus said, "If a man love me, he will keep my words: and my Father will love him, and we will come unto him, and make our abode with him." (John 14:23)

It is through the abiding presence of God that we have access to all that we need and desire and these promises tell us how to have His presence ever with us.

James tells us that "*every* good gift and *every* perfect gift is from above, and cometh down from the Father of lights, with whom is no variableness, neither shadow of turning." (James 1:17) We can therefore be certain that nothing good will come from Satan and that we must look to our Heavenly Father to obtain what we desire.

Paul told Timothy, "God hath not given us the spirit of fear; but of power, and of love, and of a sound mind." (II Tim. 1:7) Therefore, let us turn to God to obtain that positive confession that is required to exercise our faith and that perfect love that makes it work.

For years I went about knowing that I must make positive confessions if I were to receive the answers to my prayers, but I did not know how to really have those confessions *be truth*. You see, I believed legally and intellectually that God would answer my prayers because His written word said He would. He had told me in His written word that, if I believed that Jesus was God's Son, He and the Father would dwell in me, and I believed. He had said that if I kept Jesus's words, (and I had) He would make His abode with me. He had also said that if I kept His words, I could have whatever I asked, but I just could not seem to get the answers to my prayers even when I knew I had kept the commandments that He had given.

Oh, how frustrating it is to desire something and know God *can* supply it, and not know if *He will*: to be sure in your heart that you have kept His commandments to the limit of your understanding of them, and to still be unable to know in your heart that your prayers have been heard and that the answer is on the way!

I went on seeing the sick prayed for, and some healed and some not. I heard prayers for financial needs, and some were met and some were not. I heard prayers for lost loved ones, and some were saved and some were not. I heard prayers for peace of mind, and some were set free and some were not. As I began to search for the truth that would resolve this, it seemed that I would explode under the pressure of needing to know the answers, and yet no answer came. That is . . . until I *began to keep those words of the Lord that were not commandments, but were rather, His present instructions to me, and I began to listen to Him speak to me His assurance and His directions of how to receive the answers to my prayers.*

Paul said, "We through the Spirit wait for the hope of righteousness by faith. For in Jesus Christ neither circumcision availeth anything, nor uncircumcision; but faith which worketh by love". (Gal. 5:7) You see, we cannot earn God's blessings, but we must believe His words and follow, not only in obedience to His commandments, but, in trust, we must follow His *presently spoken instructions*. I began to see and understand that although I had kept his commandments and was, therefore, pleasing to Him, I still must *hear* His *instructions*. Only then was I enabled to begin to apply these scriptures that I had been taught by the faith teachers.

Mark 11:22 declares, "Have faith in God". These were Jesus's own words and this was a direct commandment to you and to me. A more apt and literal translation would be "Have God's faith." Jesus then said, "I say unto you, that whosoever shall say unto this mountain, be thou removed, and be thou cast into the sea; and shall not doubt in his heart, but shall believe that those things which he saith shall come to pass; he shall have whatsoever he saith." It is easy enough to speak to the mountain, but it is impossible to believe in the heart that it will perform one's command *until we have God's own faith!* There is only one place to get God's faith and only one way to receive it. We must get it from God himself, and we receive it *when He speaks it to us!* I am sure that God thought about framing the worlds and creating all things a long time before they were manifested, but nothing happened until he finished thinking and started *speaking*. It was not until God said, "Light be," that Light was!

God's statement was a confession of God's faith and when God's faith is confessed, it is God's word that goes forth! He has told us that when His word goes forth it will surely perform that which He has sent it to do.

Therefore, I submit to you, that the way to have a positive confession is to let that confession be from God and not from your own vain imagination.

Jesus said, "It is the spirit that quickeneth; the flesh profiteth nothing. The *words* that I speak unto you, *they* are spirit and *they* are life."

CHAPTER 10

How Mistakes Might Arise
In Trying To Hear God

The question has been asked, "Have you ever thought you had allowed God to speak through you, using your voice with which to speak audibly, only to later discover that you had been misled and that you had evidently only imagined that God spoke, or else that you had heard some other voice, because the thing did not come to pass?"

The answer is "No!" This does not imply, however, that I have not had difficulty keeping faith, and on occasion have allowed doubt to creep in and hinder or stop God's work in my behalf. You see, God honors and rewards faith exercised in love; and, as His word declares, "If we love him we will keep his words." This means both His words that are written in the Bible and the words He speaks to us now.

Since it is faith that God honors and since that faith is only worked by love; and since we know we love Him when we keep His commandments and they are not grievous, it necessarily follows that we must firmly hold on to every word of God to receive His full blessing. If we turn loose of His word and begin to doubt, we will stay God's hand from acting in our behalf.

I was in Port Lavaca, Texas with the traveling Christian book store and was enjoying an excellent reception. Sales were good, and for two days the ministry had been fruitful. I was thoroughly enjoying the company of my many friends there, and I really wanted to stay another day. I felt that I needed to move to another city, however, since the sales seemed to have nearly reached their end.

Before going to bed I asked the Lord if I should stay another day or move and He answered, "Thou art to stay in Port Lavaca until 4:00 tomorrow afternoon. At that time you are to go to Edna, Texas and serve my people there for they have desire of thee. Thou art to stay in Edna until 3:00 o'clock the following afternoon, then move to your meeting in Victoria."

I replied, "Thank you, Lord, for your instruction, and I will leave here at 4:00 o'clock tomorrow afternoon".

The next day was tremendous. I was blessed with sales and a young charismatic minister in Port Lavaca, brought me a much needed new pair of shoes. Things were great.

As 4 o'clock approached, the pastor of the Assembly of God Church at Point Comfort, which is only six miles from Port Lavaca, came into the trailer and encouraged me to come to his church on my way to Edna, Texas. He informed me that Brother F. E. Ward would be speaking. I love this precious man of God and covet the opportunity to be under his ministry whenever possible; so, without consulting God, I agreed to stop for the service on my way to Edna.

I left Port Lavaca at 4 o'clock as God had instructed and drove to Point Comfort. I opened the book trailer expecting to sell a number of books, and to my surprise nothing sold. After the service the people visited the trailer and stayed late. Still, nothing sold and at about eleven o'clock the pastor and Brother Ward suggested that we all go back to Port Lavaca and get something to eat. By the time we were finished eating, I realized that I would be much too late getting into Edna to feel like opening the trailer early in the morning and I was due in Victoria, Texas at 4 o'clock the next afternoon. Therefore, it only made sense (carnal sense) to go straight to Victoria and to postpone my trip to Edna.

I opened the trailer in Victoria about 11 o'clock the next morning and from then until 4 o'clock that afternoon I saw no one. I then moved my trailer to the auditorium where I was due to be at 4 o'clock that afternoon, and business resumed as normal. My disobeying God had cost me a full day's sales and I really needed them badly.

When I entered the meeting at Victoria, one of the first people I met was a pastor from Edna. He exclaimed, "Oh, Wes, I was praying that you would be in Edna today. I really needed some fellowship and our people needed books. Not only had I disobeyed God, I had disappointed and blocked my brother's prayers.

God has never failed to perform His word nor will He ever fail. We sometimes fail to allow God to speak, and often quickly forget the details of His answers to us. When we think we may have heard some voice other than God's, after specifically asking God to speak to us by His Holy Spirit, we are doubting His promise to us and are surely opening the door for Satan to speak or for our own vain reasoning to take over.

God's word is firm in its statement, "How much more will the heavenly Father give the Holy Spirit to them that ask Him". We must not doubt this promise if we are to effectively converse with God in any form, audible or otherwise.

I have found two sure ways to *prevent* God freely giving verbal guidance:

1. Asking Him for guidance with the intention of obeying only if His answer suits my desires. He demands complete willingness to obey His answer or He will generally refrain from speaking, as an act of mercy.

2. Failing to approach Him in a proper way, so as to block my own imagination or Satan's spirit from entering the picture. We must be careful to make certain that our mind is fixed on God and that we address Him in such a way as to bind Satan and to bind our own spirit from answering us.

Having become willing to obey, we will not

block God's answer and having directly asked Him to speak to us, we may be sure He will answer and *will not* let another spirit answer first.

Every occasion that I have failed to receive the things God spoke to me has been preceded by doubt on my part. God did His part .... I failed to respond by doing my part!

CHAPTER 11

The Price Of Ignoring God

One morning as I went to prayer, God spoke, saying, "Son, you know Billy Graham is to open his crusade in Texas Stadium at Irving tomorrow evening and you should get permission to record the crusade and sell the tapes."

I said to myself, "Now *that* has to be my imagination. Billy Graham has his own tape ministry and he wouldn't let anyone record a crusade and offer the tapes to the public!" I subsequently dismissed the subject from my mind and went about the business of trying to keep our ministerial boat afloat financially. It wasn't long however, until someone said to me, "Why don't you record Billy Graham's crusade?" Then a couple of hours later another said, "Hey Wes, Billy Graham is in town, why don't you record him?"

The next day another friend remarked, "It sure

would be wonderful if you were to record the crusade. I would love to have the tapes."

I dismissed each of these statements as being the vain imaginations of man, but little by little the weight of them began to work on me until, by the middle of the week, when the crusade was half over, my curiosity got the best of me, and I began to suspect that I had made a mistake.

I picked up the phone and called the crusade headquarters and asked who I should talk with concerning this matter. I was immediately put in touch with Mr. Cliff Barrows, and another gentleman, and to my surprise, their reaction was as follows: "Oh, Mr. Bush, you should have contacted us sooner. We have been contemplating starting a tape ministry for Mr. Graham, but we have done nothing as yet. Had you contacted us earlier, we would have printed order forms, furnished a booth, and announced that you were recording; however, we feel that we could not do this properly at this point in the crusade since we could not make the public understand why there were no recordings of the first four nights, and there isn't sufficient time now to make the arrangements."

My heart nearly broke within me, for I was in desperate need of a financial break at that time and I realized that recordings of these meetings could have sold many thousands due to the enormous crowds attending the crusade.

Ignoring God is costly!

SECTION III

Benefits Of Hearing God

CHAPTER 12

The Blessing Of Following God

While I was driving through Waco, Texas one afternoon, God prompted me to realize that I was to remain there for a while. I felt in a real hurry to be on my way, having been on the road for nearly two weeks. However, the hunger to stay in Waco became greater and I realized that I could not ignore it, and I asked God to tell me what He wanted me to do. It seemed as if He did not hear me, yet I knew I could not leave.

I went to a restaurant and sat there meditating over what possible purpose could be served by my delaying in Waco. I began to tick off mentally all the people I knew in town and proceeded to attempt to reach them by phone one by one. Not even one of them answered their phone. I began to feel as if I should visit the parents of my closest friend, but I had visited them only a few weeks before and could not understand why God would have me return so soon.

As the desire to see them grew within me, I again asked the Lord to speak and direct me. This time He answered, "I would have thee to visit Mrs. Kelton, for I have a work for you to do there". I didn't bother to call because it was now dusk and I needed to be on my way home. Using the phone seemed like a waste of time anyway since God had spoken.

When Mrs. Kelton answered the door she didn't even say, 'Hello'. She exclaimed, "Wesley, you will never believe what is happening in the Baptist church! She then led me inside and through the house to the den where we found another good Baptist lady from across the street. She was sitting on the floor in the midst of a scattering of Bibles, concordances, books, and the pages of a letter.

Both of these precious saints began talking at once, trying to tell me about the wonderful miracles that were taking place in the Baptist church. The pieces of this verbal puzzle were coming at me so rapidly that I could not assimilate them, nor could I get a word in, to try to establish order.

After about thirty minutes of this uncontrolled, excited, relating of miracles and healings, I still did not know where these things had occurred or when. I was finally able to slow these delightfully, excited Baptist ladies down, long enough to get an answer.

They handed me a letter from the daughter of Mrs. Kelton's friend who was sitting on the floor. The letter contained many beautifully written pages and told of a great many miracles and healing that had occurred at the Mt. Franklin Baptist Church in El Paso, Texas. The testimony was so clear, God-inspired, and faith-filled, that I too rejoiced as I read it.

The letter related that Charles and Frances Hunter, two precious friends of mine, had been invited to speak in El Paso, and had encouraged the folks at the Mt. Franklin Baptist Church to pray for a miracle and to announce that they were going to have a miracle service that Tuesday night.

A little girl who desperately wanted God to give her a miracle, learned about the forthcoming miracle service. She had cerebral palsy and could not walk. She was confined to a brace and for a long time had been without hope of ever recovering.

The church was packed that Tuesday night, with a great many people standing, but one in the congregation could not stand, for she had removed her braces before coming to the church in anticipation of a miracle.

As Frances and Charles Hunter spoke under the anointing of God, faith began to swell in the people. Then God spoke to both Frances and Charles at the same time and they knew that they must pray for the little girl. When they laid hands on her, she literally became a new little girl, no longer plagued by the dread thing that had crippled her, she stood completely whole. Praise the name of Jesus!

This was but one of the tremendous things that took place in that service, as God did exceeding abundantly more than those people had thought or imagined when they had prayed for a miracle service.

I knew as I read the letter that this was why God had wanted me to see Mrs. Kelton, for I was to be with Frances Hunter the following week in Arlington at a Women's Aglow Fellowship meeting. I knew I was to take the letter to her and that she would receive it with great joy.

When I handed the letter to Frances she was both amazed and overjoyed. She informed me that she was writing a book of testimonies of the things that were happening in the Church today and she wanted to use the letter in her book.

She has since published the book and many thousands have shared the wonderful miracles as they read "Since Jesus Passed By."

What a blessing it is to be an instrument in God's hands to serve and edify the Body of Christ. What a privilege to be directed by the Heavenly Father and see His hand at work.

CHAPTER 13

Total Victory Follows Listening And Obeying

We were invited to supply the book display and to record the Full Gospel Business Men's Regional Convention in Denver, Colorado in August of 1973. This was just after we had completed the assembly of our new, mobile Christian bookstore. The store consists of a 30′ trailer that houses the store, pulled by a 25′ motor coach, serving as both power supply and living quarters. The entire vehicle is as large as a very large tractor-trailer truck and measures 55' in overall length. This would, obviously, normally present quite a parking problem in the downtown sections of the major cities, but when God directs, every need is supplied.

Recognizing the potential problems in parking such a vehicle in downtown Denver, we decided to leave home a few days early, in order to arrive there on the Sunday before the Wednesday the convention was to open. We stopped at the Denver Hilton Hotel and conferred with the man in charge that day, concerning where to park. He informed us that we would have ample space in the commercial dock area of the hotel. However, he also warned that it would be a somewhat undesirable place in which to stay while at the convention, since it was in the underground level of the hotel and there would be a constant stream of trucks loading and unloading in that area.

We were overjoyed that we had so quickly solved our parking problems and assured him that we would make out just fine so far as the living part was concerned. We left the city and spent three glorious days communing with God in Rocky Mountain National Park amid some of God's most beautiful creation.

The joy of the Lord was upon us when we returned to Denver Wednesday at noon, expecting to simply park, unload the trailer and display our books in plenty of time for the convention. To our dismay, we discovered that we had talked to the wrong person, and that we could not remain in the commercial area of the hotel beyond 8:00 that evening, since three conventions would be leaving the hotel at the same time, and three others arriving.

Hoping to be able to unload in advance we sought a place to leave our merchandise, only to learn that there would be no room for it until the other conventions vacated and that wouldn't be until after 8:00 p.m. This would necessitate our unloading 5,000 pounds of books outside the hotel and carrying them in, which would be no small chore.

Immediately we began seeking a nearby place to park. After investigating the adjacent parking lots, we finally found a place in one of them where we could park and require only two spaces. Another advantage was that we would only have to cross one street to get to the hotel. Since we could use dollies to haul the books, it would be possible to unload in time to get set up for the first meeting.

We contacted the owner of the parking lot and he informed us that he would not let us park where we wished, but would let us park in his other lot across the street. He also stated that we would require *seven spaces* and that the cost would be $2.50 each day for *each space*. His sign read, 'open 24 hours per day. Maximum rate $1.50 per day.' As he told me this, the Spirit of the Lord spoke through me and simply said, "No, thank you." I was stunned and so was the man. I turned dumbfounded, and began to walk away, wondering to myself what I could possibly do now. There simply was no other place to park and I had to do something right away.

My oldest son asked, "What are you going to do now, Daddy?" I found myself replying (as the Holy Ghost gave the utterance), "Why, call City Hall, of course."

The telephones in the hotel were busy and I anxiously waited to get access to one to find out what God was going to do. I called the number I thought would connect me with the right person and was given another number. Upon calling this number, I was told that I needed to talk to someone else, and was given another number. This number too was wrong, but the party on the other end of the line informed me that I needed to talk to the head traffic engineer of Denver, but that it would do me no good since Denver is very strict on the parking of commercial vehicles and I would not be allowed to park at the curb. I insisted on speaking, however, and was given the number.

When the head traffic engineer answered, I told him my predicament, and he asked, "How long is the vehicle?" When I answered him, he exclaimed, "Fifty-five feet! Man, *you're not even supposed to be* in downtown Denver. We allow no vehicles longer than 38 feet in the downtown area of Denver during daylight hours!"

I apologized and asked what I should do. He replied, "I would advise you to remove the vehicle promptly before you are ticketed. Does the vehicle have any advertising on the sides?" When I told him that three entire sides of the book trailer were covered with signs 7' high, he sputtered, "That seals it, there is absolutely nothing I can do to help you. We allow only 2 sq. ft. of advertising on any side of a vehicle in the daylight hours."

My heart was sinking and doubt was almost upon me, when I heard him ask, "What convention are you here for?" When I told him that I was to serve the Full Gospel Business Men's Regional Convention, he shouted, "Praise God! I know those guys, they're a great bunch of men!" I attend church at Calvary Temple where many of them attend. Come to think of it, I might be able to make some concessions. You are a non-profit organization in the ministry of the Lord. I'll tell you what, go and choose the spot you want most. You will require 3 meters. Get the numbers off the base of the meters and call me back. I will send someone to put a red sack over them to reserve them for you and when the spaces are empty you will be able to park there." Glory be to God, my Father had again provided!

I nearly hung up, but was reminded that I had not written the man's number and did not know how to call him back. As he gave me the number I was frantically searching for something to write with, and had nothing. I looked down and to my amazement there lay a ballpoint pen tucked neatly between the bottom of the telephone and the shelf beneath. Hallelujah! What provision!

Having written down the telephone number, I went out and selected a choice spot and recorded the three meter numbers. The meters I chose were just outside the commercial dock area and had a downhill ramp right into the freight elevator that would lift our merchandise to the display area. This was the very spot I would have chosen had I been given my original choice. All I would need to do is turn to my right as I left the commercial area and pull along the curb. This would put my doors at the curb and allow me to unload with ease.

There was just one small problem. I would be facing the wrong direction on a six-lane, one-way, street, but that's no problem for a God who can place a Holy Ghost baptized traffic chief in the right place at the right time!

I bounded back to the telephone, dialed the number and joyfully gave my brother the numbers of the meters. He said he would send someone to flag the meters and I would be able to park there soon. I then told him of my need to park facing the wrong direction, and he said, I'm sorry, but that is not in my department. However, I can tell you that you cannot get that permission. We don't even allow our City vehicles to do that except in cases of extreme emergency."

I thanked him and invited him to visit the convention and began frantically trying to find someone who could help me locate a place to unload my merchandise since I could not possibly unload it into the street facing six lanes of fast-moving traffic. No one could be found. The man I needed to see could not be located by even the manager of the hotel. Everyone searched for him and time was running out. We finally located him at 5 P.M. I told him my situation and he said, "Man, there is nothing I can do to help you. We have no vacant spot to put your things. We must get permission for you to park the wrong way along the street".

He then called the police and they informed him that the only man who could give that permission had left at 5 o'clock and that he could not be reached until 8 a.m. The young man then said, "Look, we must turn this guy the wrong way! Send a patrolman to park him, and as soon as he gets unloaded we will call you and you can turn him back around." The Police agreed to do this and I assumed my problems were over. God had provided again.

We were standing on the curb waiting for the patrol car but still in some distress. There was a truck parked in a loading zone between my spaces and the entrance to the commercial dock. There was also a car parked in one of the rear spaces and we were told it had been there all day and money had not been deposited in the meter. I was apprehensive, since I feared that the least thing might cost us our right to park there.

Just as the patrol car rolled into the commercial dock area, a man got into the car behind the one that was illegally parked and in our back space, and drove it off. We walked back to the car that was still in our space, reached through the window, put it in neutral and gently eased it into the vacated space, thus a totally clear area in which to park. God had done it again!

The patrol car whizzed out into the street with sirens screaming, and red lights flashing, just in time for the traffic light to change and release the six-lane flood of onrushing traffic. The drivers angrily shook their fists and honked their horns and threateningly nudged the patrol car with their bumpers, too impatient to allow us to park. As we rolled to a stop, the patrol car backed into the loading zone to let the angry mob pass, as he could not possibly turn around. I have never seen such an angry demonstration. Nor, I believe, had the patrolman who sat slumped in a daze afterwards. I pleaded with him, "Sir, you can see my predicament. I must stay here four days, getting in and out of our coach and trailer. We will be fortunate to survive, if we have to enter and exit into that angry mass of traffic."

He handed me his card, and solemnly agreed, "If anyone gives you a ticket, call me and I will waive it."

Glory be to God! Prase His Holy Name! Hearing and obey God brings total victory.

The man at the parking lot who had tried to take advantage of us was required to watch us for four days, as we enjoyed the spot of our choice. As it worked out, we weren't even charged for the parking! The traffic engineer had refused to send us a bill for the use of the parking spaces, since we were a non-profit organization on a mission for God. To make the victory even more complete, my dime was returned each of the four times that I called to reach the traffic engineer. When I had called to give him the parking meter numbers, I tried to get the same telephone, since it had been returning my dimes. However, that phone was in use, and I was forced to use another. When I hung up the second phone's receiver, the phone clicked and my dime was returned. Praise God! Satan was utterly cast down. The total victory came, through *hearing, haerkening, trusting,* and *obeying* God and it didn't cost even a dime!

CHAPTER 14

*What We May Ask
And Expect To Receive*

A very small child sometimes has very big desires. Desires that cannot be granted by his father because the child would be incapable of handling the things desired, and in some cases might even be harmed by them. As the child grows in stature and maturity, however, his father can begin to grant more and more freedom of choice to the child. Christian babes are likewise unable to handle all the things that they desire and the Heavenly Father has given guidelines of growth that show us the pattern He follows in allowing us the things we desire of Him.

John tells us, "This is the confidence that we have in him, that, if *we ask anything according to his will*, he heareth us: and if we know that he hear us, *whatsoever we ask*, we know that we have the petitions that we desire of him". (IJn. 5:14-15)

He also said, "Beloved, if our heart condemn us not, then have we confidence toward God. And *whatsoever we ask*, we receive of Him, because we keep his commandments, and do those things that are pleasing in his sight." (IJn. 3:21,22)

How like little children we really are as young Christians. Have you ever noticed how a small child, in total innocence, will ask for things he could not have, and how disappointed and sometimes angry he becomes when denied his desire? Have you also noticed that in order to cause a small child to obey his father's commands, a little chastening may have to be applied?

We too, often ask for that which is outside the Father's will and many times we react like the child when we fail to get what we desire. We also disobey God's commandments because our own desires dictate what we do and say instead of our Father's desires.

Hebrews 12:4-8 tells us, "Ye have not resisted unto blood, striving against sin. And ye have forgotten the exhortation which speaketh unto you as unto children, My son, despise not thou the chastening of the Lord, nor faint when thou are rebuked of him: For whom the Lord loveth he chasteneth, and scourgeth every son whom he receiveth. If ye endure chastening, God dealeth with you as with sons; for what son is he whom the father chasteneth not? But if ye be without chastisement, whereof all are partakers, then are ye bastards, and not sons."

God chastises His children to purge them of their disobedience and until we have been completely purged, He must limit His answers to our prayers for we will pray amiss without realizing it and, therefore, not in accordance with His will.

While we are yet children, the Scripture says, "Ye ask, and receive not, because ye ask amiss, that ye may consume it upon your lusts". (James 4:3)

Matthew 18:18-19 declares, in Jesus' own words, "Verily, I say unto you, *whatsoever* ye shall bind on earth shall be bound in heaven: and *whatsoever* ye shall loose on earth shall be loosed in heaven. Again I say unto you, that if two of you shall agree on earth *as touching anything* that they shall ask, it shall be done for them of my father which is in heaven. For where two or three are gathered together in my name, there am I in the midst of them."

I submit unto you beloved, that *nothing* is withheld from those who love God, keep His words, seek in faith, ask in accordance with His will, and knock at *His door* for the answers.

God has made full and adequate provision for every need and every desire of His children. Won't you avail yourself of His abundance today?

CHAPTER 15

Hearing God Speak Peace Concerning Lost Loved Ones

Jesus said in His own words, "As Moses lifted up the serpent in the wilderness, even so must the Son of man be lifted up: that whosoever believeth in him should not perish, but have eternal life.

"For God so loved the world, that he gave his only begotten Son, that whosoever believeth in him should not perish, but have everlasting life. For God sent not his Son into the world to condemn the world; but that the world through him might be saved.

"He that believeth on him is not condemned: but he that believeth not is condemned already, because he hath not believed in the name of the only begotten Son of God. And this is the condemnation, that light is come into the world, and men loved darkness rather than light, because their deeds were evil.

"For everyone that doeth evil hateth the light, neither cometh to the light, lest his deeds should be reproved. But he that doeth truth cometh to the light that his deeds may be made manifest, that they are wrought in God."

This passage of scripture clearly sets forth God's

desire that all men be saved and also definitely establishes the pathway that leads to salvation that none who reads it should miss the positively stated basis for eternal life.

The problem comes in getting our loved ones to see the truth of Christ's message and to desire the light which Jesus both speaks of and is, rather than darkness. Often it seems, only a very traumatic experience enables them to see Christ. We apparently can stay the hand of providence with our prayers of faith, to such a degree that our loved ones are shielded from such an experience. Whereas, if we were to release them completely into God's hands, in total trust that He *will* bring them through to perfect salvation, He then could allow situations and circumstances to arise to manipulate them into such a 'crossroad experience'.

We all too often pray effective prayers of protection over our loved ones which do stay the hand of God. We pray, "God, keep them safe; God, keep them healthy; God, provide them a good job; God, make their home life happy; God, protect their children"; and on and on. Each of these requests is both logical and desirable but really only *after* God has been allowed to exercise His will in their lives by bringing them unto salvation: we know from Jesus's own words that *it is* God's will that all should have eternal life.

An elderly lady asked me to pray with her for her husband who claimed to be a Christian, but loved darkness rather than light. I agreed to pray for him, but God spoke to me before I could pray and told me to ask her a question. He said, "Ask her if she is willing that I slay him and destroy his flesh that he might be saved and thereby be with her in heaven?" After hearing the question, the sister replied that she would be willing for God to take him as he was quite elderly and she wanted him saved for eternity. God then prompted me to ask her to agree with me in the following prayer, and God gave me the utterance for the words that were prayed: "Dear God, we recognize you as our Father and that you desire only that which is good for us. You know the sincere desire of this your daughter, to have her husband saved and prepared to meet you. She has placed him upon the altar and has said that you can take his life if it pleases you, only please save him for eternity. We remove all the protective fences we have built around him with our prayers of faith and simply place him in your hands. We trust you father, to save his eternal life. Your Word said that Jesus breathed on the disciples and said unto them, "Receive ye the Holy Ghost, whosoever sins ye remit, they are remitted unto them; and whosoever sins ye retain, they are retained". (John 20:23) We agree to lift Christ up to him in all respects. We will show love when he evinces hatred. We will show mercy when he is vengeful. We will show righteousness when he is sinful. We will show kindness when he is angry. In short, Father, we will love him not for what he is today, but for what he will be when you have finished with him.

"We ask you now, Lord, to send your angels, whom you made ministering spirits, to surround him and to arrange his circumstances to be such that he will see his need and will know that only Jesus can meet it, and will cry out to him for salvation. We ask you to save him, baptize him with the Holy Ghost and with *fire*. In Jesus' Name we ask all these things.

"Now, because your word declares that 'what things soever ye desire, when ye pray, believe that ye receive them, and ye shall have them' (Mark 11:24); we do believe that the things we have asked are already done; and our confession from this day forward is that this husband *is* saved, baptized in the Holy Ghost and in *fire* and will shortly manifest all these things in his thoughts, words, and deeds. Amen."

The Lord then spoke these words to the lady through me, saying, "For yea, and I have heard thy plea this day, my daughter, and my word has surely declared that I desire the salvation of your husband. For surely I will save him and will answer thy request for thou hast asked in accordance with my will; not demanding the impossible, but requesting that which I made possible, yea, even before I made man, made I it possible to redeem him when he fell."

"Go therefore and keep thy words and lift up my Son, and I will surely save thy husband. Keep thy conversation righteous, for my Word hath declared, 'Wives, be in subjection to your own husbands; that, if any obey not the Word, they also may without the Word be won by the conversation of the wives; while they behold your chaste conversation coupled with fear' (I Peter 3:1). Fear not the things which seem to come upon him for his harm, but rather know that it is my will and only by my will that these things are allowed to happen; for, you have given him to me and he is mine; and, not anything will happen that I allow not to happen that he might be saved. Go in peace my daughter, for surely I the Lord thy God have spoken to thee this day."

Hallelujah, we had an answer from God and began to openly confess that this husband was saved, baptized in the Holy Ghost and in *fire*, and that he would shortly show us the evidence in thought, word and deed.

Three days after we prayed this prayer, the husband had a severe heart attack which nearly killed him. A few days later God miraculously healed him and raised him up, full of God's love, and testifying to God's saving him and healing his body. Praise be unto His holy name!

I submit unto you, my beloved brothers and sisters in Christ, that we do not have to be worried over our loved ones, but that we should be confident of their salvation. We can surely have total peace when we have placed them in God's hands without strings and have set His ministering spirits at work to lead them to Christ whom we have been faithful to lift up by loving them, not for what they are, but for what they will be when God is finished with them. We can have complete confidence and peace when we allow God to speak His answer to us, through us.

CHAPTER 16

How Your Hearing God Affects Others

Intercession for others is a real ministry and one that every mature Christian freely engages in out of love for the brethren and for the lost. Jesus breathed on the Disciples and instructed, "Receive ye the Holy Ghost: whosesoever sins ye remit, they are remitted unto them; and whosesoever sins ye retain, they are retained." (Jn. 20:22,23) This action brought with it both the instruction and the enablement for the saints to properly act as intercessors.

When one in the Body of Christ has a fault or a need, the others in the Body have both the *power* and the *obligation* to minister to that situation in love.

If one sins a terrible sin, we should never let Satan have him. We should, rather, forgive him, remitting his sin in faith because of love and watch God change both the one at fault and the circumstances of the fault. "Brethren, if a man be overtaken in a fault, ye which are spiritual, restore such an one in the spirit of meekness; considering thyself, lest thou also be tempted. Bear ye one another's burdens, and so fulfill the law of Christ." (Gal. 6:1-2)

"Moreover, if thy brother shall trespass against thee, go and tell him his fault between thee and him alone: if he shall hear thee, thou hast gained thy brother. But, if he will not hear thee, then take with thee one or two more, that in the mouth of two or three witnesses every word may be established. And if he shall neglect to hear them, tell it unto the church: but if he neglect to hear the church, let him be unto thee as an heathen man and a publican."

"Verily I say unto you, whatsoever ye shall bind on earth shall be bound in heaven: and whatsoever ye shall loose on earth shall be loosed in heaven.

"Again I say unto you, that if two of you shall agree on earth as touching anything *that they shall ask*, it shall be done for them of my Father which is in heaven. For where two or three are gathered together in my name, there am I in the midst of them." (Matt. 18:15-20)

I declare unto you my brethren that we have a singular responsibility not to let those we know and love suffer and perish. We are to restore them and save them from the clutches of the Wicked One. Jesus gave us the *privilege* of remitting their sin and thus with intercession staying the hand of God's wrath. It is not God's will that any should perish but that all might have everlasting life and that more abundantly.

Not only are we to forgive and restore them

from sin; but, my beloved, we are to interceed for their health and raise them up from their beds of affliction and, yes, even from the bed of death.

In this behalf, I would declare to you that it is not enough to merely desire that they be set free from the chains of sin and death. We must put those desires into action. But how and unto what action?

I am not smart enough to know what to do, for example, to raise one from the dead, nor to turn one from his wickedness; nor am I wise enough to know how to use even the limited knowledge I might have. I need to go to the One who has *all* knowledge and *all* wisdom and *all* power and set the matter before Him and then to obey His instructions (verbal or otherwise) if I am to see the wicked changed and the dead raised.

The evening of June 26th, 1971 was a solemn night for my wife and myself. We were in deep financial need with $2,000.00 of bills coming due the first of the month and nothing on hand. We were to attend the Albuquerque, New Mexico Regional Convention of the Full Gospel Business Men's Fellowship, to officially record the meetings and to furnish the book table. We were scheduled to leave for Albuquerque the following day. We had no hope that enough income could be generated through this meeting to fill our need, since the meeting was to be attended by less than 600 people. So small a crowd could scarcely be expected to buy anywhere near $2,000.00 of books and tapes.

We were discussing the dilemma when the doorbell rang. I rejoiced in my soul, when I opened the door to find Sherwin and Leah McCurdy, two of our faith-filled friends awaiting entry. I just knew that God had sent these precious people to pray for our need.

I had no sooner closed the door than the bell rang again. To my amazement I opened the door to Jack and Leta Rae Carney, with the joy of the Lord radiating from their faces.

Hallelujah! Now I knew we would have the funds we needed, for we had believers present who loved us and would agree with us that God would supply our need. I explained the desperate nature of our situation to these wonderful brethren and informed them of the amount of our need. We then began to pray. As soon as we began, God began speaking to me in that still, small voice, saying, "Wes, Brother and Sister McCurdy did not come to pray for your need, for I had already heard your prayers concerning it and the bills will be paid. They came to get you to agree in prayer with them that I would heal and raise up the man they have been visiting in the hospital."

I knew that God had told me the truth, for I recalled then that the McCurdys had been coming to Arlington every evening for the past eight nights to sit with and pray for a man who had been in a deep coma for nine days. He had been diagnosed as having the always-fatal "staph meningitis". The doctors said there was no chance of his living, and that even if he were to live he could never be more than a "vegetable". Oh how selfish I had been. How much greater was that man's need than mine!

The Lord directed, "Son, tell Sherwin and Jack that it is my desire that you anoint a fresh cloth with oil in Jesus's name; and, then you and Jack anoint Sherwin with oil, thus anointing him to deliver the cloth and minister healing to the dying man." I related this God-expressed desire to Sherwin and Jack. We proceeded to anoint both the cloth and Sherwin and then began to praise and rejoice over the battle that had been won! For God had spoken and the victory was ours!

Sherwin and Leah immediately took the cloth to the hospital and placed it upon the dying man. Sherwin then began to instruct the unconscious man regarding healing, and to minister the word to him that God had spoken concerning raising him up. Glory to God! The man responded! His hands began to move. For the first time in almost nine days, there was a sign of life. Sherwin began to talk to him, telling him each time the particular sign to make with his hand to signify his answer. The conversation was lengthy, determining that the man knew Jesus as his saviour and had resisted a ministry God had established for his life. He agreed that he would move into that ministry when his body was whole, in response to God's love.

Sherwin and Leah later left the hospital rejoicing, as did the man's wife for she now had a living husband rather than widowhood. Praise be to His Holy Name!

The next morning upon returning to the hospital the wife was stunned when informed that the doctor had just examined her husband and had pronounced him dead! What a tremendous shock! She could not . . . . . would not . . believe it; for God had spoken *life* and God never lied.

She exclaimed, "Where is the cloth that was placed on my husband last evening?"

"Oh, we removed it right after you left. He was not to have anything touching him, you see", she was told.

"You put that cloth back on him!" she ordered as she tearfully turned toward the chapel to pray.

The cloth was placed upon the *already dead* man, and seemingly nothing happened. Later a nurse entered the room to get the chart from which to prepare the death certificate. She exploded from the room shouting, "He's alive! He's alive! That man's *alive* in there!" God had done it again. By nightfall the man was sitting up in bed, quite upset with the doctor because he could not be released to return to his home. Sherwin had a powerful testimony for the Albuquerque Convention, and I had peace in my heart because I knew my need was to be met.

We delighted in the wonders that God performed during the Convention and in watching God supply $2,050.00 in sales in spite of the fact that all the main speakers brought and sold their own books, which would normally have excluded us completely.

Our God is sufficient to every task. However,

He does expect us to be *His instruments* to do His divine work in accordance with His *present* instruction. When we follow Him in this way, we see God's work in our behalf each time.

God's written word tells us what God has done, will do, and can do. His present spoken word tells us when, where and how we may become partakers of these blessings in our lives.

CHAPTER 17

How Hearing God Relates To Spiritual Gifts

Paul said, "I would that ye all spake with tongues, but rather that ye prophesied: for greater is he that prophesieth than he that speaketh with tongues, except he interpret, that the church may receive edifying". (I Cor. 14:5)

When Paul made this declaration, he intimated that *any believer* could prophesy if he allowed himself to be used of God willingly. Paul knew that many believers were not practiced candidates for being used by God in the manifestation of spiritual gifts and he desired that they be, not only willing to be used, but qualified and equipped to be used.

His statement in the 12th verse of the 14th Chapter of I Corinthians clearly sets this forth,

"Even so ye, forasmuch as ye are zealous of spiritual gifts, seek that ye may *excel* to the edifying of the church. Wherefore let him that speaketh in an unknown tongue pray that he may interpret." Paul very clearly understood the relationship of spiritual inspiration to thought; and of thought to speech; and he desired that the Corinthians have a *true conversational relationship with God the Father*. He knew that until this conversational relationship was established, no completely effectual manifestation of God's gifts could be seen in a believer.

In I Corinthians, chapter 12, he tells us that the source of spiritual inspiration determines the words that a man speaks. "Now concerning spiritual gifts, brethren, I would not have you ignorant. Ye know that ye were Gentiles, carried away unto these dumb idols, *even as ye were led*." (I Cor. 12:1-2) Led by what? Why, led by the spirit of Satan, of course, for the next verse states, "Wherefore I give you to understand, that no man speaking by the Spirit of God calleth Jesus accursed: and that no man can say that Jesus is the Lord, but by the Holy Ghost".

So we see that Paul clearly understood the value of *divine inspiration* of our thoughts in the regulation of our words and deeds and he subsequently shows us that this spiritual inspiration operates the spiritual gifts.

He went on to say, "Now there are diversities of gifts, but the same Spirit (Holy Spirit). And there are differences of administrations, but the same Lord (Jesus). And there are diversities of operations, but it is the same God (the Father) which worketh all in all. But the manifestation of the Spirit is given to *every* man to profit withal." Does the term *every man* include you? I submit that it does *if you are willing*.

He further states, "For to one is given by the Spirit the *word* of wisdom; to another the *word* of knowledge by the same spirit; to another faith (the *word* of faith for it is the confessed word of God that does the work) by the same Spirit; to another the gifts of healing by the same Spirit; to another the working of miracles; to another prophecy; to another discerning of spirits; to another divers kinds of tongues; to another the interpretation of tongues: but all these worketh that one and the selfsame Spirit, dividing to every man *severally* (more than one gift at a time) as he will."

But all these worketh that selfsame Spirit . . . the Holy Spirit! You will recall our previous observation that the pattern God uses in speaking to us is that the Holy Spirit inspires us to think thoughts which when spoken without contaminating them with rationalization and our own thoughts . . . are God's words and will surely come to pass.

In Acts 10:38 we see, "How God anointed (inspired) Jesus of Nazareth with the Holy Ghost and with power: who went about doing good, and healing all that were oppressed of the devil for God was with him".

I would submit unto you therefore, that to be used by God to manifest or minister spiritual gifts, one must first, receive God's *inspiration;* second, think God's *thoughts;* and third, both speak God's *words* and act God's *actions*. To be a candidate for this to take place in your life, you need only believe and be willing. Paul, however, went on to say, "seek to excel". Therefore we should practice the one relationship that will best equip us to be used by God when the Spirit moves. That relationship is talking to God in the privacy of our own prayer closet, and listening to Him as He instructs us; speaking audibly to us, *through us.*

Many people who have never experienced this type of conversational relationship have been moved upon by God to manifest a spiritual gift, and have been frightened to inaction or silence because they were unaccustomed to this form of spiritual relationship.

One who is accustomed to conversing with God and hearing Him speak through the voice of their own 'temple' is not so shaken when God moves upon them to prophesy or speak a word of knowledge, faith, or wisdom, and will usually give the word in a sure, authoritative manner instead of a halting, stumbling, or a loud, screeching oration.

God is pleased with those who receive of His abundance in complete trust and faith. Won't you converse with Him each day, practicing to become a qualified candidate to be used of God in the operation of His spiritual gifts?

What a tremendous blessing it is to have God prophesy through you, thereby edifying, exhorting, and comforting the Body. What a blessed prospect to be used as God's instrument to carry the Gospel of the Kingdom to one of another language as God gives the utterance because no interpreter is present. What a blessed hope that one would be used to minister a gift of healing or a miracle to someone in need. All these are yours when you are willing and when you believe. Hear Him, hearken to Him, trust Him, and obey Him.

"For I know the thoughts that I think toward you, saith the Lord, thoughts of peace, and not evil, to give you an *expected* end. Then shall ye call upon me, and ye shall go and pray unto me, and I will hearken unto you. And ye shall seek me, and find me, when ye shall search for me with all your heart. And I *will* be found of you, saith the Lord". (Jeremiah 29:11-14)

SECTION IV

God Speaking Through Prophecy

CHAPTER 18

Who Should Prophesy?

Paul tells us in I Corinthians 14:31, "*Ye may all prophesy one by one, that all may learn, and all may be comforted*".

Again, in I Corinthians 14:4-5 he says, "he that prophesieth speaketh unto men to edification, and exhortation, and comfort. He that speaketh in an unknown tongue edifieth himself; but he that prophesieth edifieth the church. *I would that ye all spake with tongues, but rather that ye prophesied:* for greater is he that prophesieth than he that speaketh with tongues, except he interpret, that the church may receive edifying."

We see that Paul fully accepted and taught that *any believer* could and should prophesy; just as he desired that all believers speak in tongues. He also gave clear instructions that all were permitted to prophesy one by one, implying that more than one would prophesy in any given gathering.

He explains in I Corinthians 14:23-25 why we should prophesy, "If therefore the whole church be come together into one place, and all speak with tongues, and there come in those that are unlearned, or unbelievers, will they not say that ye are mad? But if all prophesy, and there come in one that believeth not, or one unlearned, he is convinced of all, he is judged of all: and *thus are the secrets of his heart made manifest;* and so falling down on his face, he will worship God, and report that God is in you of a truth."

We see then that all can and should prophesy; that prophesying manifests the secrets of the heart; that prophesying edifies the church; that prophesying leads the hearers to worship God; and that prophesying reveals to the unlearned or to the unbeliever the God in us!

CHAPTER 19

Where Does Prophecy Come From?

Jesus said in Matthew 12:34, "Oh generation of vipers, how can ye, being evil, speak good things? For *out of the abundance of the heart the mouth speaketh.* A good man out of the good treasure of the heart bringeth forth good things: and an evil man out of the evil treasure bringeth forth evil things. But I say unto you, that every idle word that man shall speak, they shall give account thereof in the day of judgement. For by thy words thou shalt be justified, and by thy words thou shalt be condemned."

So, we see that out of the abundance of the heart the mouth speaketh. To prophesy one must speak; therefore, we may assume that prophecy originates in the heart, but, how is the prophecy conceived in the heart? We know that prophesying is good to edify, exhort, and comfort the hearer. We may assume then that it certainly is not conceived by Satan since he will not edify but will destroy instead.

Remember Jesus' words, "O generation of vipers, how can ye, being evil, speak good things?" Hereby know we that true prophesying does not originate in Satan, but in God; from whom all good things come.

We must be aware, however, that Satan does send forth false prophets who prophesy lies against God. Jeremiah 29:21 says, "Thus saith the Lord of hosts, the God of Israel, of Ahab the son of Kolaiah, and of Zedekiah the son of Maaseiah, which prophesy a lie unto you in my name; behold I will deliver them into the hand of Nebuchadrezzar, king of Babylon, and he shall slay them before your eyes".

The penalty the false prophet must pay is a stiff one and God intended that the people not forget it. He said in Jeremiah 29:22, "and of them shall be taken up a curse by all the captivity of Judah which are in Babylon, saying, the Lord make thee like Zedekiah and like Ahab, whom the king of Babylon roasted in the fire; because they have committed villany in Israel, and have committed adultery with their neighbors' wives, and *have spoken lying words in my name*, which I have not commanded them; even I know, and am a witness, saith the Lord."

The ultimate test of any prophecy to determine if it be a true or a false prophecy is whether it comes to pass. God declares in Ezekiel 12:25 "I am the Lord; I will speak, and the word that I shall speak *shall come to pass*".

Again in Deuteronomy 18:20-22, we see the penalty of false prophecy and the result, "The prophet which shall presume to speak a word in my name, which I have not commanded him to speak, or that shall speak in the name of other gods, even that prophet shall die. And if thou say in thine heart, How shall we know the word which the Lord hath spoken? When a prophet speaketh in the name of the Lord, if *the thing follow not, nor come to pass*, that is the thing which the *Lord hath not spoken*, but the prophet hath spoken it presumptuously: thou shalt not be afraid of him."

CHAPTER 20

Pre-Testing Your Own Prophecy

In view of the penalty for falsely prophesying, we naturally have an extreme desire to know that the voice we hear when we prophesy is truly God speaking. We have several promises in God's Word which reassure us and let us move comfortably in this dimension.

Numbers 23:19 declares, "God is not a man, that he should *lie:* neither the son of man that he should repent." In face of that declaration let us then appropriate God's promise given in Luke 11:11, "If a son shall ask bread of any of you that is a father, will he give him a stone? or if he ask a fish, will he for a fish give a serpent? or if he shall ask an egg, will he offer him a scorpion? If ye then, being evil, know how to give good gifts unto your children: how much more shall your heavenly Father give the Holy Spirit to them that ask him?"

Having appropriated these two promises we may be certain that we will hear no other voice than God's voice when we ask the Father to speak through us.

Luke 11:9 instructs us to ask, "I say unto you, ask, and it shall be given you; seek, and ye shall find; knock, and it shall be opened unto you."

Luke 11:10 tell us what then to expect. "For everyone that asketh receiveth; and he that seeketh findeth; and to him that knocketh it shall be opened".

By now it should be clear that when we desire to prophesy, we may do so. All we need to do is ask (and allow) God to speak to us and through us, and He will surely speak; but how do we know when He is speaking? In order to understand this, we must first understand the way speech comes to be.

Man is a spirit, a soul, and a body. Man's spirit desires, and to fulfill those desires, gives inspiration or direction to his soul which thinks thoughts, plans plans, makes decisions, and then directs the body to act or to speak in fulfillment of his desires.

Every word that a man speaks is first preceeded by a thought. Every thought a man thinks is inspired by one of these spirits: Satan's spirit, man's spirit, or God's spirit.

When Satan inspires thought, the thought will be evil; the words that come forth from such thought will be Satan's words; and Satan's words will always bring destruction.

When man's own spirit inspires thought, the thought will be man's thought. Romans 8:20 tells us that "the creature (man) was made subject to vanity*, not willingly, but by reason of him who hath subjected the same in hope". Since man is subject to vanity, any thought inspired by man's spirit will likely be vain, the words that come forth from those thoughts will be void, and the subsequent actions will be selfish.

When God's spirit (The Holy Spirit) inspires thought; the thought will be God's thought and the words which issue forth from such thought will be God's words. Thoughts that are inspired by God will always be good and the words they bring forth will always be creative. God tells us in

---

*The Greek word Paul used for vanity was "Mataiotes" which literally interpreted means: inutility, transientness, moral depravity. Hence we see man's uncertain spirit made manifest.

Isaiah 55:11, "My word, that goeth forth out of my mouth: it shall not return unto me void, but it shall accomplish that which I please, and it shall prosper in the thing whereto I sent it."

Jeremiah 17:5-11 declares our need to rely on God's inspiration rather than ours, for it says, "thus saith the Lord; *cursed be the man that trusteth in man*, and maketh flesh his arm, and whose heart departeth from the Lord. For he shall be like the heath in the desert, and shall not see when good cometh; but shall inhabit the parched places in the wilderness, in a salt land and not inhabited. *"Blessed is the man that trusteth in the Lord*, and whose hope the Lord is. For he shall be as a tree planted by the waters, and that spreadeth out her roots by the river, and shall not see when heat cometh, but her leaf shall be green; and shall not be careful in the year of draught, neither shall cease from yielding fruit.

"The heart (human spirit) is deceitful above all things, and desperately wicked: who can know it? I the Lord search the heart, I try the reins, even to give every man according to his ways, and according to the fruit of his doings. As a partridge sitteth on eggs, and hatcheth them not; so he that getteth riches, and not by right, shall leave them in the midst of his days, and at his end shall be a fool."

Paul's writing in the second chapter of I Corinthians so thoroughly agrees with Jeremiah that we cannot possibly miss this principle in demonstration for he declares, "I, brethren, when I came to you, came not with excellency of speech or of wisdom, declaring unto you the testimony of God. For I determined not to know anything among you, save Jesus Christ, and him crucified.

"And I was with you in weakness, and in fear, and in much trembling. And my speech and my preaching was not with enticing words of man's wisdom, but in demonstration of the Spirit and of power: that your faith should not stand in the wisdom of men, but in the power of God.

"Howbeit we speak wisdom among them that are perfect (mature): yet not the wisdom of this world, nor of the princes of this world, that come to naught: but we speak the wisdom of God in a mystery, even the hidden wisdom, which God ordained before the world unto our glory: which none of the princes of this world knew: for had they known it, they would not have crucified the Lord of glory.

"But as it is written, eye hath not seen, nor ear heard, neither has it entered into the heart (spirit) of man, the things which God hath prepared for them that love him. But God hath revealed them unto us by his Spirit: for the Spirit (of God) searcheth all things, yea, the deep things of God.

"For what man knoweth the things of a man, save the spirit of man which is in him? Even so the things of God knoweth no man but the Spirit of God.

"Now we (the mature saints spoken of in verse

6) have received, not the spirit of the world, but the spirit which is of God; that we might know the things that are freely given to us of God. Which things also we speak, not in the words which man's wisdom teacheth, but which the Holy Ghost teacheth; comparing spiritual things with spiritual.

"But the natural man receiveth not the things of the Spirit of God: for they are foolishness unto him: neither can he know them because they are spiritually discerned. But he that is spiritual (i.e. in Christ) judgeth all things, yet he himself is judged of no man. For who hath known the mind of the Lord, that he may instruct him? But we have the mind of Christ."

Oh, how revealing are these words of Paul, that so beautifully reveal the need for the spiritual discernment that will let one know and recognize God's inspiration in contrast to the inspiration of man or Satan; for, if we would fulfill the will of God, we must allow *Him* to inspire our thoughts and be willing to speak those selfsame thoughts out loud that the hearers (including ourselves) may be edified, exhorted, and comforted. Such inspired conversation will always reap a harvest of abundant life.

CHAPTER 21

How You May Prophesy

Remember the Father's words, "If you know how to give good gifts to your children; how much more will the heavenly father give the Holy Spirit to them that ask?" When we desire to prophesy, we are desiring God to speak His words through us; therefore, we are asking His Holy Spirit to inspire our thoughts so that we may speak the words of those thoughts and thereby speak His words.

Because He said He would give us the Holy Spirit when we asked and that He would not give us a substitute, we can be sure that *He will not allow Satan's spirit to inspire* our thoughts and that *He will not let our own spirit inspire* our thoughts but, *His Holy Spirit will inspire* our thoughts and we will be hearing God speak as we speak the words of those thoughts out loud.

We must enter into this relationship with total confidence in His word; knowing that the very first thought that comes to us after we have asked the Holy Spirit to speak to us *must* (cannot possibly be otherwise) *be God's thought*, and that when we speak the words of that thought *we will be speaking God's words;* not one word of which will return void.

We should *practice* this relationship in the privacy of our own prayer closet; thereby receiving God's instruction for us and the verbal answer to our prayers before we see the physical evidence manifested. This type of conversational relationship with God will produce great joy and extreme peace for we will be literally following God's instruction for our individual lives rather than walking in what might seem to be the semi-darkness of a general precept; and we know that as we obey God, we receive His blessing. When we converse with God in this audible fashion we are talking to God in the same manner that many of the men of God recorded in the Bible talked with Him.

Prophesying actually does not differ from this conversational relationship with God except that prophecy is normally directed toward someone other than the person prophesying; although the one speaking may be included within the scope of the prophecy.

God will speak through any willing person. He awaits such a person's invitation to the Holy Spirit to speak through him, that He may edify, exhort, and comfort the church. We should all be willing to allow God's Holy Spirit to speak through us. We should enter into any gathering both *desiring* and *expecting* God to use us in this capacity. When we approach a meeting in this attitude, He will see our willingness and speak through us when He desires to speak.

We need only to be willing and to have confidence that when we ask His Holy Spirit to speak, no other spirit can manifest itself *first* through us, for God will not allow it.

CHAPTER 22

Stumbling Blocks To Prophesying

Failure to accept the truth that God will prevent another spirit from speaking when we have asked God's Holy Spirit to speak, will surely be a stumbling block to some people. We must stand upon God's promise by faith and know that only God's Spirit will be allowed to inspire our thoughts when we have asked God to speak to us or through us, or we will never be able to prophesy with confidence.

To overcome the fear that Satan might speak, or your own spirit might speak, bind both those spirits and ask God the Father expressly to prevent any spirit inspiring your thoughts except His Holy Spirit. Having asked God in this fashion to speak, you can be assured that you will not be allowed to hear any other voice than His. You can also be certain that the first thought that enters your mind will be a God-inspired thought: A thought which when spoken will become God's inspired creative word and will surely come to pass.

Another common stumbling block is desiring or expecting God to inspire whole sentences before you begin to speak them. Were he to do this you would mix the inspired thought of God with your own thought and when the words came forth they would *no longer be God's word* but would have become *man's word*. God wishes to speak directly through you and will usually give you only two or three words at a time. When you speak the first words by faith, you will find that the rest of His words will automatically follow. When you speak in this fashion you are allowing God's creative word to be spoken through you and you can be sure that it will edify, exhort, and comfort the hearer.

Satan does not desire for any child of God to maintain this speaking relationship with God, and will do everything he can to distract and draw one's attention away from conversing with God. For this reason one should make a positive effort to spend time alone with God. Select a private place to pray. Allow sufficient time to have a lengthy conversation with God, even as much as two or three hours if possible. Set aside all pressing problems by realizing that God is going to take care of them and that any that he does not take care of immediately will be none the worse for waiting.

Approach God with confidence that He wants

to instruct you, teach you, guide you, and comfort you. God wants to talk to you. Renew your faith that His Spirit is the first voice you will hear when you stand on His promise of the Holy Spirit. Ask sincere, intelligent questions and expect positive clear answers. Ask for actual needs to be met and expect to hear His directions and assurances concerning how to get them met.

Ask one thing at a time and when you have asked meditate and wait for His answer. The *first* thought you have will be His answer. Be willing to trust the answer and obey His instructions. Speak His answer right out loud as it is given to you so you will hear it with your mind as well as with your heart.

Hebrews 8:10 says, "This is the covenant that I will make with the house of Israel after those days, saith the Lord; I will put my laws into their mind, and write them in their hearts: and I will be to them a God, and they shall be to me a people."

God wants to put His words in your mind. When you speak the words he inspires in you, as you receive them in your heart, the words become a part of your memory. To further seal them in your mind you may wish to write down the words, as writing often assists in imbedding things in our memory.

CHAPTER 23

Why Prophesy?

Isaiah 55 declares, "Ho, everyone that thirsteth, come ye to the waters, (Spirits of God), and he that hath no money; come ye, buy, and eat; yea, come, buy wine (Holy Spirit) and milk (Word of God) without money and without price. Wherefore do ye spend money for that which is not bread (carnal bread)? and your labour for that which satisfieth not? *hearken* dilligently unto me, and eat ye that which is good (Bread of Life), and let your soul delight itself in fatness. *Incline your ear*, and come unto me: *hear*, and your soul shall live; and I will make an everlasting covenant with you, even the sure mercies of David. Behold, I have given him for a witness to the people, a leader and commander to the people. Behold, thou shalt call a nation that thou knowest not, and nations that knew not thee shall run unto thee because of the Lord thy God, and for the Holy One of Israel; for he hath glorified thee.

"Seek ye the Lord while he may be found, call ye upon him while he is near: Let the wicked forsake his way, and the unrighteous man his thoughts: and let him return unto the Lord, and he will have mercy upon him; and to our God, for he will abundantly pardon.

"For my thoughts are not your thoughts, neither are your ways my ways, saith the Lord. For as the heavens are higher than the earth, so are my ways higher than your ways, and my thoughts than your thoughts. For as the rain cometh down, and the snow from heaven, and returneth not thither, but watereth the earth, and maketh it bring forth and bud, that it may give seed (written word) to the sower, and bread (spoken word) to the eater: So shall my word be that goeth forth out of my mouth: it shall not return unto me void, but it shall accomplish that which I please, and it shall prosper in the thing whereto I sent it. For *ye* shall go out with joy, and be led forth with peace: the mountains (congregations) and the hills (gatherings) shall break forth before you into singing, and all the trees of the field (Saints) shall clap their hands. Instead of the thorn (hypocrite) shall come up the fir tree (worthy Christian), and instead of the brier (reprobate) shall come up the myrtle tree (Bride adorned): and it shall be to the Lord for a name, for an everlasting sign that shall not be cut off."

If you wish to be an instrument of blessing, exhortation and edification, yield completely to God and let Him inspire your thoughts. Then speak forth *His* words as He inspires them; that the congregation may be blessed and joyfully clap their hands for having heard God speak.   Amen

SECTION V

God Speaking Through Power (Fire)

CHAPTER 24

About The Fire

A few years after I received the Holy Ghost, I reached a crossroads that demanded a decision. I could either continue down the pathway I was walking, praying in tongues daily, building myself up in the most Holy Faith; or, I could seek the higher pathway of power upon which the apostles had begun to walk on the day of Pentecost.

You see, I had the indwelling Spirit of truth, the Holy Ghost, but I did not have the power to stand in the face of 3000 murderous Jews and preach the Gospel of the Kingdom as Peter did on the day of Pentecost.

Peter knew that those Jews were likely to kill him, but he preached to them anyway. For that was what the Lord had said to do. Only a few days before he had denied Christ three times and that perhaps only to save face: and now, instead of being filled with fear of death and fear of reproach, he was boldly proclaiming God's word before 3000 or more Jews who he was sure would kill him. What had made the difference? Was it the Holy Ghost? Was it speaking in tongues?

If it *was* the Holy Ghost and speaking in tongues; why then didn't *I* have the power to face reproach or death or poverty to proclaim the message of the Kingdom that was burning within me? Why would I turn away from the instruction of the Lord when He would speak to me in a restaurant and say, "Speak to the man at that table about me for I have prepared him to receive your witness." Why, if the power was *in* the Holy Ghost or *in* tongues, would I say, "Oh no Lord, this is a public place, and besides, he wouldn't want to hear it from me anyway."? Why would I refuse to reprove a person of a sin that would destroy him when I had the truth and the truth would set him free?

The answer was simple. I had the Holy Ghost, but I did not have the power! I prayed in unknown tongues by the hour and would just fill up with faith, but I did not have the power to exercise that faith in the face of unpleasant circumstances.

I was used by the Lord to speak messages in tongues and to interpret messages in tongues; but, I did not move freely in this ministry to the church due to fear of reproach. I simply did not have the *power* that Jesus had told the Apostles to tarry for. Jesus used a singular, very traumatic incident to cause me to realize the significance of this lack of power in my life. I shall never forget that experience.

I was listening to a minister distort the words of God before a congregation of about 300 people one Sunday morning. He was building a case for licentious living, stating that physical, fleshly sins had no significance in our relationships with God, that God does not look on the outside but only upon the heart. He was mentioning fornication, lying, stealing, adultery, and many of the other sins that God declared would prevent a man from entering the kingdom of heaven, and ascribing to them a mere earthly significance rather than a spiritual one as well.

I knew the people in the congregation well, and I could spot many of those who were guilty of the various sins being named. Their faces were beaming as this false teacher tickled their ears and seared callouses over their consciences. Then God spoke to me, "Wes, read the 56th Chapter of Isaiah to the people when he is finished."

"But, Lord," I exclaimed, "if I do that I will be thrown out of the church and separated from the people who are believing these lies and I will never be able to deal with them again!" What a lie of the devil I had spoken! To even imagine that I could answer the situation with my words and my wisdom bordered upon insanity, yet I had hearkened to the devil instead of to God and had fallen into disobedience.

God replied, "The man will open the floor for any to speak who desire to do so. When he does I desire that you read the 56th Chapter of Isaiah. You need not say anything or take any responsibility; just read that chapter."

I sat hoping that the man would not offer anyone the opportunity to speak; but he closed his remarks with, "If anyone takes exception to what I have said, let him stand and state his piece."

Oh, my God! My God! I did not have the power to simply rise and speak God's written word: even in a church!

I would be reproached!

I would be separated from my friends!

I would be thrown out of the church!

I, I, I, I, I, I, ...

But what about those poor, lost, deceived souls who might perish for my silence?

I left the sanctuary full of grief and remained griefstricken until one by one I was able to personally contact those people and to witness to the truth. However, my heart continued to cry out within me, "Oh God, *where* is the power?"

The disciples had found it while tarrying in the upper room. I then decided to also tarry—at the crossroads until I was endowed with power from on high, and could move on into the work of the Lord even in the face of opposition!

CHAPTER 25

Search For The Fire

The search for the truth took me into the Bible where I saw in Acts 10:38 "How God anointed

Jesus of Nazareth with the Holy Ghost *and with* power: who went about doing good."

I saw in Matthew 3:11 where John the Baptist said, "I indeed baptize you with water unto repentance: but he that cometh after me is mightier than I, whose shoes I am not worthy to bear: he shall baptize you with the Holy Ghost, *AND WITH FIRE*: Whose fan is in his hand, and he will thoroughly purge his floor, and gather his wheat into the garner; but he will burn up the chaff with unquenchable fire."

I saw in St. Luke 3:16 where John said, "I indeed baptize you with water; but one mightier than I cometh, the latchet of whose shoes I am not worthy to unloose: he shall baptize you with the Holy Ghost *AND WITH FIRE*: whose fan is in his hand, and he will thoroughly purge his floor and will gather the wheat into his garner; but the chaff he will burn with fire unquenchable."

Praise God, I really began to realize who the baptizer was, although I was still uncertain of what the power was, when Jesus began to minister the Word to me in that still small voice. He said, "Remember how I told the Disciples in John the 14th Chapter to 'keep my commandments and I will pray the Father, and he shall give you another comforter, that he may abide with you forever; even the Spirit of truth; whom the world cannot receive, because it seeth him not, neither knoweth him: but ye know him: for he dwelleth with you and shall be in you?'

He said, "Remember I also said, "these things I have spoken unto you, being present with you. But the Comforter, which is the Holy Ghost, whom the Father will send in my name, he shall teach you all things, and bring all things to your remembrance, whatsoever I have said unto you. (John 14:25, 26) And remember I said that "When the comforter is come, whom I will send unto you from the Father, *even the Spirit of truth*, which proceedeth from the Father, he shall testify of me: and ye also shall bear witness because ye have been with me from the beginning."

The Spirit of Truth! The Spirit of Truth! The Comforter, The Holy Ghost, even the *Spirit of Truth*!

I said, "But God, the Spirit of truth was not the spirit that settled on Christ when he came up out of the water at John's baptism. That Spirit was your Spirit, the Spirit of God!"

We are told in Matthew 3:16, and "Jesus, when he was baptized, went up straightway out of the water: and, lo, the heavens were opened unto him, and he saw the Spirit of God descending like a dove, and lighting upon him: and lo a voice from heaven, saying, This is my beloved Son, in whom I am well pleased."

Again in Mark 1:9-11, "And it came to pass in those days, that Jesus came from Nazareth of Galilee, and was baptized of John in Jordan. And straightway coming up out of the water, he saw the heavens opened, and the Spirit (capitalized signifying the Spirit of God) like a dove descending upon him: and there came a voice from heaven, saying, Thou art my beloved Son, in whom I am well pleased."

John tells us in John 1:32-34, "And John bare record, saying, I saw the Spirit (capitalized again signifying the Spirit of God the Father) descending from heaven like a dove, and it abode upon him. And I knew him not: but he that sent me to baptize with water, the same said unto me, Upon whom thou shalt see the Spirit descending, and remaining on him, the same is he which baptizeth with the Holy Ghost. And I saw, and bare record that this is the Son of God."

I remembered Jesus's answer to the high priest who asked him if he were the Son of God, "Thou hast said: nevertheless I say unto you, Hereafter shall ye see the Son of Man sitting on the right hand of *power*, and coming in the clouds of heaven." (Matt. 26:64)

Now everyone knows that Jesus is seated on the right hand of God the Father; therefore, *the Father and power had to be the same!*

Praise God, now I could see that the power or fire was ministered by God the Father and not by the Holy Ghost and I knew in part what I lacked. The knowledge overwhelmed me that the tri-une God when fulfilling the office of the Son ministered everlasting life unto me; when fulfilling the office of the Holy Ghost ministered the truth to me, which truth includes the knowledge and understanding of Jesus's words and the true witness of his indwelling presence in my life; and, when fulfilling the office of the Father, he would surely minister power unto me—the *power* to overcome the fear of poverty, sickness, death and reproach. Yes, the *power* to stand free—free from the Adamic curse.

I could clearly see that Adam had come under the bondage of death when, in the third chapter of Genesis, God had told him that if he partook of the forbidden fruit he should surely die, and thus came death into the inheritance of natural man. I could see that sickness was a part of the curse in the dying process, but even more, a part of the increase of sorrow in childbearing and farming; for, ungodly sorrow is a form of mental illness and often leads one into physical sickness. That Adam came under bondage to poverty was made apparent in God's statement that the ground was cursed for his sake and that in sorrow would he eat of it all his days; and, that in the sweat of his face he would eat his bread. Reproach was to remain ever present with him from the very moment he knew his nakedness and was ashamed.

In contemplating the state of my personal weaknesses, I realized that although I had accepted Jesus Christ as my Saviour and had been washed to regeneration by His Word; and, had been renewed in my mind by the Holy Ghost, I had not been quickened in body and delivered from *my* fleshly ties to the Adamic curse. *My spirit* was willing but *my flesh* was weak.

I heard Jesus himself as He took the Bible and began to read the book of Isaiah to the men in the temple, "The Spirit of the Lord* is upon me, because he hath anointed me to preach the Gospel to the poor; he hath sent me to heal the brokenhearted, to preach deliverance to the captives, and recovering of sight to the blind, to set at liberty them that are bruised, to preach the acceptable year of the Lord." (Luke 4:18,19)

I remembered Samson as he went with his father and mother to the vinyard of Timnath: and behold a young lion roared against him. "And the Spirit of the Lord came mightily upon him, and he rent him as he would have rent a kid, and he had nothing in his hand." (Judges 14:5-6)

I remembered that Judges 15:14 declared that "when he (Samson) came unto Lehi, the Philistines shouted against him: and the Spirit of the Lord came mightily upon him, and the cords that were upon his arms became as flax that was burnt with fire, and his bands loosed from off his hands. And he found a new jawbone of an ass, and put

---

*The original Greek word for Lord literally translated means *"Supreme Authority"*. It is interesting to note that the Spirit of the Lord and the Spirit of God are one and the same, although the Greek word for Lord is Kurios, meaning "Supreme in Authority" or "Controller", and the Greek word for God, as used in the term Spirit of God, is Theos, meaning "the supreme divinity". i.e. We know the Father to be both Supreme Authority and Supreme Diety, hence "Supreme power".

forth his hand, and took it, and slew a thousand men therewith."

I heard Micah's cry against the prophets, and his declaration in Micah 3:8, *"Truly I am full of power by the Spirit of the Lord, and of judgment, and of might, to declare unto Jacob his transgression, and to Israel his sin."*

The Spirit of the Lord! The Spirit of the Lord! Oh, how I hungered for the ministry of the Spirit of the Lord! For I knew that in that Spirit was the fullness of the Power of the Godhead bodily, and that with the anointing of that Spirit, I would become free from the fear of poverty, the fear of death, the fear of sickness, and the fear of reproach. I would have *power* to completely overcome the Adamic Curse.

CHAPTER 26

How To Find The Fire

How was I to get this Power? How for that matter had I obtained the Spirit of Life in Christ Jesus and the Spirit of Truth in the Holy Ghost? What would be the manifestation that would let me know of a certainty that I had really received the ministry of the Spirit of the Lord when it came? More and more questions flooded in upon me as I pondered this subject.

Again the word of the Lord opened to me and reminded me of Jesus' words to the believing Jews in John 2:31-32, "If ye continue in my word then are ye my disciples indeed; and ye shall know the truth, and the truth shall make you free." Free from what? Why, free from death; for just before that he had told these same Jews, "Ye shall die in your sins; for if ye believe not that I am he, ye shall die in your sins."

The Word had revealed to me through Paul, in Romans 8:9, "But ye are not in the flesh, but in the Spirit, if so be that the *Spirit of God* dwell in you." And Romans 8:11 cried out to me that if the same Spirit "that raised up Jesus from the dead, dwell in you, he that raised up Christ from the dead shall also quicken your mortal bodies by his Spirit that dwelleth in you."

I had abided in Jesus and He in me; and, I was quickened to remember that he came to dwell with me when I accepted him into my spirit (heart) by faith.

He had baptized me with the Holy Ghost (Spirit of Truth) when I had reached out to Him by faith and put on the mind of Christ, and had given me the glorious assurance that I had truly been *BAPTIZED* by Him with the Holy Ghost when He let me speak in an unknown tongue.

Now by that same Holy Ghost He had revealed to me that I could be set free from the curse of sin and death and could know the assurance of my immortality by simply inviting the Spirit of God (the Father) to anoint me; and that I was free to invite Him (the Father) to dwell in me for I had sanctified the temple of my flesh to Him and cleansed it from all unrighteousness of which I was aware and had kept His commandments by and through the grace of Jesus Christ.

Jesus said, "If a man love me, he will keep my words: and my Father will love him, and *we* will come unto him, and make *our abode* with him" (John 14:23).

I reached out to the Father and invited him to dwell in me, fully expecting guns to go off and bells to ring and many mighty manifestations to take place; but literally nothing happened that I could discern at that time. Then, little by little, I began to realize that a great and wonderful transformation had taken place in me. I began to know—*to know without any doubt*, that the Spirit of the Lord *was upon me* and as He did unto Christ He did unto me. He literally drove me into the wilderness and unleashed Satan to tempt me in ways I never dreamed I could be tempted; but the joy of the Lord *is* my strength and I *can* do all things through Christ Jesus who strengtheneth me, and Satan has lost his battle in the name of Jesus.

With each test comes a fresh anointing of the Spirit of the Lord upon me to enable me to overcome by *His power*.

With each test a little more of the iniquity that is in my flesh is being burned out. For His fan is truly in His hand and He is thoroughly purging His threshing floor until all that is undesirable to Him vanishes and only that which is pleasing to Him shall remain.

Yea, though I walk through the valley of the shadow of death, I will fear no evil for the Spirit of the Lord is with me and I have been given the *power* to overcome and to become a son of God. "For as many as are led by the *Spirit of God*, they are the sons of God. For ye have not received the spirit of bondage again to fear, but ye have received the spirit of adoption, whereby we cry, Abba, Father. The Spirit (capitalized to signify the Spirit of God) itself beareth witness with our spirit; that we are the children of God: and if children, then heirs; heirs of God, and joint-heirs with Christ; if so be that we suffer with him, that we may be also glorified together." (Rom. 8:14-17) Praise be to His Holy Name!

Are you at the crossroad, wondering which path to take? Have you received the Holy Ghost but not received the *power*? Ask in faith for the same anointing that God gave Jesus of Nazareth when He anointed Him with the Holy Ghost *AND WITH POWER*; and by faith walk in that anointing, declaring unto all men by the confession of your mouth that the Spirit of the Lord is upon you and hath anointed you to become a son of God. Then too, begin to show forth by your actions, that you are *truly transformed* into the kingdom of Light. Let it be seen that since you have been quickened to immortality, you no longer move under the curse, but have been freed from sickness, poverty, death, and reproach; for He hath anointed you with the Holy Ghost *and with Power!*

CHAPTER 27

Conclusion In Faith

If you would speak wisdom—have Faith in God
If you would speak unknown tongues—have Faith in God
If you would prophesy—have Faith in God
If you would speak faith—have Faith in God
If you would speak knowledge—have Faith in God
If you would interpret tongues—have Faith in God
If you would hear God—HAVE FAITH IN GOD

Have faith in God! "For verily I say unto you, that whosoever shall *say* unto this mountain, be thou removed, and be thou cast into the sea; and shall not doubt in his heart, but shall believe that those things which he *saith* shall come to pass; he shall have whatsoever he saith. Therefore I say unto you, what things so ever ye desire, when ye pray, believe that ye receive them, and ye shall have them." Mark 11:22-24

Again I say unto you, *Have Faith in God*, for verily I say unto you, that whosoever shall say unto God, *SPEAK TO ME BY YOUR HOLY SPIRIT GIVING ME DIRECTION FOR MY LIFE AND VERBAL ANSWERS TO MY PRAYERS;* and shall not doubt in his heart, but *shall believe* that those things which he *saith* shall come to pass; he shall have whatsoever he *saith*. Therefore I say unto you, if ye desire to hear God's audible answers to your prayers when ye pray, *believe* that ye hear God's answer both in your heart and as God speaks it audibly with your voice.

Again I say, have faith in God, from whom cometh *all* good things.

Have faith in God!

Have faith!

Have:

> to hold in the hand or in control; own; possess; experience; undergo; understand; know; declare; state; master; receive; obtain; consume; bear; beget; perform; carry on; engage in; cause to be; feel; show; permit; tolerate; *AND TO OVERCOME!*
>
> Webster's New World Dictionary
> Maranatha!

CHAPTER 28

Key Questions And Answers

1. *How do I hear God speak?*
Although the Bible tells us a few instances when God did speak out of the thunderings and the lightnings, this is not the general way in which He has spoken. The more frequent way in which He speaks is through inspired thought; the still small voice we hear in our mind as we seek Him and pray.

2. *How do I recognize His voice?*
God's Spirit is gentle and peaceable and easily entreated; therefore you can expect His voice to be the same. The testimony of all who talk to Him is that He speaks in a still, small, voice that is gentle but both sure and firm.

3. *How can I be sure that it is Him speaking to me?*
II Timothy 3:16 declares, "All scripture is given by the inspiration of God." Man's mind may receive inspiration to think and to speak thoughts from three distinct sources...God's Spirit, man's own spirit, and Satan's spirit; therefore, the source of the inspiration determines who is talking; whether man, God, or Satan. When we ask *God* to speak to us, we can be sure that no other

spirit will be allowed to inspire our *first* thought, unless we open the door for it with unbelief. Therefore, we need to ask God to speak, in faith that *only He will answer!*

4. *How can I hear Him speak to me audibly?*

When the still small voice begins to inspire your thoughts, simply allow your voice to speak those thoughts right out loud. Thus, you will have heard God with your heart and with your ears, and His words will be written both on the tables of your heart and on the table of your mind. Remember that Hebrews 8:10 tells us, "This is the covenant that I will make with the house of Israel after those days, saith the Lord, I will put my laws into their mind, and write them in their hearts: and I will be to them a God, and they shall be to me a people: and they shall not teach every man his brother, saying, Know the Lord: for *all shall know Me*, from the least to the greatest."

By this we know that it is given of God that *all* be able to talk to Him and to hear His answers.

5. *How can I know the answers to my prayers before I see the evidence with my eyes?*

If you were to invite someone to dinner, you would expect them to tell you whether they intended to come or not, lest you were to prepare in vain. When we ask God for something, we need to expect and wait for His verbal answer, lest we find ourselves anticipating in vain the thing requested of God. If we ask firmly expecting God's verbal answer and then, quietly meditate and wait for His answer, He will surely speak through our thoughts and we will know the answer without waiting for the physical evidence.

6. *I have asked God to answer, but it seems I cannot hear Him. Can you tell me why I have difficulty hearing Him?*

There are several reasons why we have difficulty hearing God:

a.) *We ask amiss.*

We say, "Lord, I want a new car. Should I buy a blue Cadillac or a red Cadillac? In asking God the question in this manner, we have not given Him the place of either King or of trusted Father. We have *told Him* that we are going to buy a new car, a Cadillac, and only asked if He would guide us on the choice of color! Our prayers should give Him more place. We should perhaps have said something like, "Father, I would like to have an automobile; my preference is a new Cadillac. If it is permissible for me to have this now, would you please help me with this decision and in determining the color? I want to be in your perfect will, so it will be okay if I don't get a car at all. I need your instruction and your guidance lest I make a mistake."

b.) *We are afraid to hear His answer.*

Many times we ask for things we know in

advance will be forbidden or that we suspect will be. Therefore, we ask the question and then close our ears so as to not hear His answer forbidding our desire. A good example of this would be praying for guidance as to whether to divorce one's spouse. We have knowledge from His word that He is displeased with divorce. Thus, in advance we can be almost certain that He will say not to divorce. We must open our hearts to Him in the area of questions whose answers don't suit us, above all, in order not to grievously sin against Him. When we allow God to instruct us we are never harmed. In the case of divorce, He will either heal the marriage or perhaps in rare cases grant the divorce.

The most important thing to remember is this: *we must hear Him, hearken to Him, trust Him,* and then *obey Him!*

c.) *We fail to really believe that He will talk to us because we feel unworthy!*

Our unworthiness is without question, but when we forgive and ask forgiveness, and when we've confessed our sins and received His forgiveness, He will impute it to us for rightousness and will hear our prayers of faith. We can then ask what we will and receive His answer if we do not doubt.

7. *How often should I expect God to speak to me?*

Enoch walked with God and was not, for God took him. Paul said to pray without ceasing. We should be so close to our Father that we ask Him about everything we do or think, and we should hear His answer before we act or speak. Jesus said, "I do that which I see the Father do and I say that which I hear Him speak." That is why His ministry was 100% effective and also explains why God's Spirit so dwelled in Him that it raised Him from the dead! (Rom. 8:11)

AN OUTSTANDING CLASSIC!!

THE BLOOD COVENANT

3.95

H. G. TURNBULL

"Those who enter into the blood covenant pledge their life blood in each other's defense, and form a more solemn bond than any which can be established by marriage or the closest natural relationships."

"The life (in the blood), not the death of the victim, has always been the important element in sacrifice."

This enlightening book pours a flood of light upon the Old and New Covenants, The Blood, the Incarnation, the Atonement, and especially *The Lord's Supper*.

A Book for those who want to go on with God and who desire *MEAT!*

DECISION TO DISCIPLESHIP, Bible Study by Roxanne Brant

The vitality and vibrancy of the ministry of the author come through in the anointed teaching sections which introduce each chapter. The explanatory material on the subjects of The Trinity, Guidance, Testing The Spirits, and Witnessing, alone could easily be well worth the price of the entire book. $3.00

MINISTERING TO THE LORD, by Roxanne Brant

The book begins "One of the main reasons for the 'power failure' today in the Christian church is that Christians have failed to minister to the Lord. The author, who herself has a miracle ministry, then proceeds to present a case for, and describes the means to minister to the Lord . . . Will revolutionize your views of worship! Rapidly becoming a bestseller. $1.50

MY PERSONAL PENTECOST, by Rev. Rodney Lensch

Thousands of copies of this powerful testimony have already touched hearts and changed lives. The account of this Missouri Synod Lutheran pastor has had a tremendous impact especially upon the Charismatic movement among Lutherans. $.70

Bestseller!!

PIGS IN THE PARLOR

$2.95

If you *really believe* JESUS delivered people from evil spirits ... Then you owe it to yourself to read this book! Learn that it *still happens today!*

This book contains a wealth of practical information for the person **interested in, planning to engage in,** or **actively engaged in** the ministry of deliverance.

It is a PRACTICAL HANDBOOK, offering valuable guidance as to determining ...

- **HOW DEMONS ENTER**
- **IF DELIVERANCE IS NEEDED**
- **HOW DELIVERANCE IS ACCOMPLISHED FOR OTHERS AND SELF**
- **HOW TO RETAIN DELIVERANCE**
- **GROUPINGS OF DEMONS** (listing those demons that are often found together).

The book also includes a chapter presenting a revelation on the problems of **SCHIZOPHRENIA** which could well revolutionize the way this subject has been traditionally viewed by the medical profession!

FOUR POWERFUL MESSAGES ON ONE HOUR CASSETTES

Additional, inspired teaching by the Author of PIGS IN THE PARLOR which amplifies and expands upon the material covered in the book.

1. WAVERING FAITH
2. THE SCHIZOPHRENIC CHURCH
3. SCHIZOPHRENIA—PART I
4. SCHIZOPHRENIA—PART II

Wherever Christian Books Are Sold: Or Use Coupon

IMPACT BOOKS, INC., 137 W. Jefferson, Kirkwood, Mo. 63122

Today's Date_____

Name_____
Address_____
City_____ State_____ Zip_____

Missouri Residents add 3% Sales Tax _____
TOTAL AMOUNT ENCLOSED $_____

Write for our complete catalog of over 500 Christian Books, Cassettes and Records.